BREAKING DOWN THE WALLS

WORLD COUNCIL OF CHURCHES
STATEMENTS AND ACTIONS ON RACISM
1948-1985

Edited by Ans J. van der Bent

Programme to Combat Racism
World Council of Churches, Geneva

Cover Design : Michael A. Dominguez
ISBN No. 2-8254-0866-2
© 1986   World Council of Churches,
150 route de Ferney, 1211 Geneva 20, Switzerland

TABLE OF CONTENTS

Director : Anwar M. Barkat
Joint Editors : PCR executive staff
Editorial Assistant : Eva Militz
Printed by : Imprimerie Marc Picarat, Geneva

PREFACE

The original edition of this booklet was published in 1980 as reference and preparatory material for a world consultation on "The Churches Responding to Racism in the 1980's". It was one of the most widely used resource materials in various regional and local consultations. It continues to be much in demand by churches and groups around the world for obvious reasons. It has been used as a study document by congregations to increase their awareness of the evil of racism and the danger that it poses for Christian faith and the unity of the human community.

The documents contained in this booklet represent not only the official position of the World Council of Churches, but also reflect the growth in thought and action in the ecumenical movement on one of the most crucial issues of our times. The centrality of the issue of racism for the life and work of the churches can hardly be over-emphasized. The churches' witness against racism and apartheid has to remain uncompromising. The conviction that racism is a perversion of God's creation and an obstacle to the church's mission is widely accepted among the family of churches. However, there are still considerable differences in what specific actions and strategies to follow in combating racism. Therefore, the struggle against racism must continue and be intensified.

The material presented here also makes abundantly clear that racism is all pervasive and worldwide. Hardly any society of part of the world is immune to the cancer of racism. It manifests itself in many different forms including tribalism, caste and discrimination against people of different ethnic origins. Even the structures and practices of the churches may not be free from the sin of racism. Confession means confrontation against the forces of evil.

The widening focus of the Programme to Combat Racism is amply illustrated here. The struggle for the Land Rights of Indigenous people has gained new urgency along with the continuing struggle against apartheid in South Africa. The violent institutions and practices of the racist regime in South Africa are no longer acceptable to the millions of blacks who are already dying for their liberty and freedom.

The reading of the original introduction by the author is still recommended as it outlines the history of the combating racism from its early beginnings. The present publication has been brought up to date with new material. We are grateful to Dr Ans van der Bent for his contribution in preparing this publication and hope that it will continue to stimulate thought and action among the churches. The actions and statements of the World Council of Churches have helped to *Breaking down the Walls* of racism in varieties of situations and have brought new awareness in their struggle against racism. We are convinced that this booklet will continue to provide guidance for the thought and actions of the churches by stating unequivocally the commitment of the WCC in combating racism.

Prof. Anwar M. Barkat
Director

INTRODUCTION TO THE SECOND EDITION

Several World Council of Churches' publications need from time to time an updating. This is also the case with this reference work which was published in 1980. Since that time a world consultation on "The Churches' Response to Racism in the 1980s" in The Netherlands in 1980, four Central Committees of the WCC and its Sixth Assembly at Vancouver, Canada in 1983 took place. These gatherings dealt with various matters concerning the combat of racism and issued new statements. They are included in this revised edition.

Also the bibliography of World Council of Churches' publications and of other recent literature has been brought up-to-date. Several books on black theology have been added.

The reading of the original foreword is still recommended as it outlines the history of the combat of racism from its early beginning onwards and the purpose of this reference work. It is hoped that this publication will serve anew as a ready source of information and orientation, and as a guide to concerted action in various parts of the world.

INTRODUCTION

This is not the first such book. The World Council of Churches published in 1965 a pamphlet titled : "Ecumenical Statements on Race Relations. Development of Ecumenical Thought on Race Relations 1937-1964". It was edited by the Secretariat on Racial and Ethnic Relations of the Department of Church and Society.

This present work contains, besides a selection of earlier statements on race relations, the World Council of Churches' more recent resolutions, statements and actions on world racism. A chronological record of what has been stated and done since 1937 precedes the collection of official documents. It provides the skeleton on which flesh has grown. Several statements are reproduced in excerpt form in order to make this collection as accessible and readable as possible.

The bibliography at the end lists only the most recent and important literature on the problem of racism and the combat against it. In "Ecumenical Statements on Race Relations (1974) and in Elisabeth Adler's book : "A Small Beginning. An Assessment of the First Five Years of the Programme to Combat Racism" (1974) bibliographies of earlier literature on racism can be consulted.

The earlier period since the Stockholm Conference on Life and Work (1925), during which a report on the "race-problem" was already discussed, was characterised by a strong optimism. It was believed that by preaching the brotherhood of men and by the spreading of modern education, race-prejudice would soon be eliminated. Hardly any attention was given to the non-rational character of overt and covert racism and to the impact of political and economic factors. The International Missionary Council, meeting at Jerusalem in 1928, adopted a statement demanding "worldwide interracial unity". Two years earlier J.H. Oldham has published a book, titled : "Christianity and the Race Problem". This pioneer in the ecumenical movement was far ahead of his time in stressing the fundamental unity of human nature, the white race's responsibility and the Church's obligation to be in the midstream of the world's life.

In the period from 1933 to 1945 the dominating issue was that of national socialist racism and more specifically antisemitism. Leaders of the ecumenical movement protested frequently against the persecution of Jews. Efforts were made to help Jews to escape. But it was not understood until it was too late that in the name of racial purity the greatest crime in history was carried out : the systematic murder of six million Jews.

In the post-war period until well into the sixties, World Council of Churches' Statements at various occasions urged its member churches to eliminate racist practices in their own ranks, to recognize their involvement in racial and ethnic tensions in the world and to denounce the violation of human rights through discrimination on grounds of race, colour and culture. Very soon the policy of apartheid in South Africa became a central issue. At almost every Central Committee meeting since 1949 the appropriate action to be taken was discussed.

In spite of many brave declarations, however, the churches and the ecumenical movement did not effectively respond to the challenges. It was not until 1959 that the World Council appointed a full-time secretary to help the member churches in dealing with problems of "interracial relations". The time had not come yet to use the term "combat against racism".

In a paper, submitted to the Notting Hill consultation on Racism in 1969, Dr W.A. Visser 't Hooft summarized the shortcomings of the pre- and post-war period as follows : "a) we have believed too much in persuasion by declarations and have not been sufficiently aware of the irrational factors of the situation; b) We have not given adequate attention to the economic factors making for racial injustice; c) We have insisted too little on the very considerable sacrifices which have to be made if racial justice is to prevail; d) We have not yet found common answers to the problem of violence and non-violence as methods of transforming present patterns and present structures."

The first General Secretary of the Council made two other observations. He noted that the race issue has not yet reached the grassroots in such a way that it has become a decisive motive in the life of the local congregations. "The real issue is not whether Christians want interracial justice and equality, but whether they are willing to pay the price for it locally." He also referred to the traditional concept of the right of resistance to tyranny, a right explicitly recognized since the Reformation. Beza, the successor of Calvin, defended this right. The Scots Confession of 1560 mentioned among the good works of Christians : the repression of (the resistance) against tyranny.

This was precisely what the Notting Hill Consultation on Racism advocated for the first time. Calling upon the World Council to make a number of steps to struggle against racism, the last step was formulated as follows : "that all else failing, the Church and churches support resistance movements, including revolutions, which are aimed at the elimination of political or economic tyranny which makes racism possible."

A few months later the Central Committee at Canterbury recommended an Ecumenical Programme to Combat Racism and outlined its five-year programme. Time was ripe now after the Fourth Assembly in Uppsala, which urged the Council "to embark on a vigorous campaign against racism", to describe the historical context in this way : "We have sadly to recognize that in spite of the battle that has been fought against racism by churches, mission agencies and Councils of Churches... racism is now a worse menace than ever. We have also sadly to confess that churches have participated in racial discrimination. Many religious institutions of the white northern world have benefited from racially exploitative economic systems. Lacking information about the possibility of developing sophisticated strategies to secure racial justice, Christians often engage in irrelevant and timid efforts to improve race relations — too little and too late."

Theologically, the Central Committee at Canterbury made an even more prophetic statement : "Our struggle is not against flesh and blood. It is against the principalities, against the powers of evil, against the deeply entrenched demonic forces of racial prejudice and hatred that we must battle. Ours is a task of exorcism. The demons operate through our social, economic and political structures. But the root of the problem is as deep as human sin, and only God's love and man's dedicated response can eradicate it. The World Council's programme is but part of that response. It is God's love and not the hatred of man that must ultimately triumph. By God's love, by the power of His Spirit, some day, soon, we shall overcome."

Despite baffling and disturbing questions raised in a study "Violence, Non-violence and the Stuggle for Social Justice", prepared by the Sub-Unit on Church and Society and commended by the Central Committee, meeting in Geneva, August 1973, to the churches for study, comment and action, and despite the absence of any scientific way to decide whether to approve or to disapprove of the Programme to Combat Racism, the World Council has tried throughout the seventies to help its member churches towards greater understanding, deeper commitment and more courageous action in the struggle for racial justice. There has been a keen awareness that "what is at stake is not just the future or a programme, but the integrity of the Church's life and the credibility of our witness to Christ as Lord of all."

The statement from the WCC Executive Committee, meeting at Arnoldshain (FRG), 1970, outlining the criteria of the Special Fund and deciding about the first grants, along with the subsequent declarations until this date are concrete in procedure and scope and are self-explanatory.

The Programme to Combat Racism has provided many opportunities for contact, consultation and dialogue with the leaders of the oppressed. An annual Programme Project List (administered separately from the Special Fund) has been developed to serve the purpose of supporting local, national and regional churches and groups as well as projects initiated by the PCR, in solidarity with the racially oppressed. Considerable research has been done and various analytical documents published that espouse the causes of marginal groups. Significant is also that investments of churches, banks and multinational corporations in South Africa were made public.

The Programme to Combat Racism has closely collaborated with other WCC sub-units, such as Faith and Order, the Commission on World Mission and Evangelism, the Commission on Interchurch Aid, Refugees and World Service, the Commission on the Churches' Participation in Development, the Commission of the Churches on International Affairs, the Office of Education, the Finance Department, Church and Society, the Communication Department and with regional ecumenical bodies such as the Christian Conference of Asia and the All African Conferences of Churches. Space does not permit us here to detail the procedures, projects and collaboration between WCC units and related organizations. Exceptional mention is made of a study guide by a conference in Arnoldshain, October 1978, jointly sponsored by the Office of Education and the Programme to Combat Racism, and published in "Racism in Children's and School Textbooks". The full report is contained in "The Slant of the Pen. Racism in Children's Books", edited by Roy Preiswerk.

What has the Programme to Combat Racism achieved so far ? What remains to be done ? How have the churches responded to it ? Will it continue to arouse controversy in the churches and evoke great interest in the mass media ? These and other questions force the Council to look into the 1980's.

In his report to the Central Committee at Kingston, Jamaica, January 1979, Philip Potter, the WCC General Secretary, highlighted the history of the struggle against racism and asked why the Special Fund has caused so much fury in some quarters. He gave several reasons why the Council has to face fierce attacks in the public media and the church press. He urged the Central Committee "to set up a process of consultation on how the churches might be involved in combatting racism in the 1980's as we review what has been done during the ten years of the PCR. In that connection we can re-examine, in the light of experience, what are the most effective instruments which can be used for achieving our declared purpose and which will engage the churches in a manner in which they can understand the issues clearly."

Dr Potter's second proposal was "that we should take seriously the call to work out some convictions and positions on political ethics as proposed in the Report of the Advisory Committee on the Search for a Just, Participatory and Sustainable Society : Focus on political ethics, i.e. : an examination of structures of power, participation and political organization on local, national and international levels."

The Central Committee agreed with these proposals to start a process of consultation with the churches in combatting racism in the coming decade. Regional ecumenical conferences and various churches in Africa, Asia, Latin America, North America and Europe have taken the initiative to organize continental and national consultations and to view newly arising issues and complications in the struggle against racism from their specific geographical and historical perspectives.

A CHRONOLOGICAL RECORD OF ECUMENICAL AND WORLD COUNCIL OF CHURCHES' RESOLUTIONS, STATEMENTS AND ACTIONS ON RACISM, 1937-1985

1937   "The Churches Survey Their Task. The Report of the Conference at Oxford, July 1937, on Church, Community and State". London : Allen & Unwin, 1937. pp. 230-235.

The Oxford conference of 1937 included in its report on "The Church and Community" a section on "The Church and Race" which set forth the fundamental concepts of Christian race relations for subsequent ecumenical gatherings. "Against racial pride, racial hatreds and persecutions, and the exploitation of other races in all their forms, the Church is called by God to set its face implacably and to utter its word unequivocally, both within and without its own borders."

1948   "Man's Disorder and God's Design". The Amsterdam Assembly Series. 5 vols. London : SCM Press, 1949.

The first WCC Assembly did not make race a separate subject, but dealt with it in several sections. Some points : "The Church cannot call society away from prejudice and segregation unless it takes steps to eliminate these practices from the Christian community." "Churches have to take a firm and vigorous stand against flagrant violation of human rights through discrimination on grounds of race, colour, culture or political conviction." A special committee on the "Christian Approach to the Jews" spoke in its report on the failure of churches fighting antisemitism which is "absolutely irreconcilable with the profession and practice of the Christian faith."

1954   "The Evanston Report. The Second Assembly of the World Council of Churches 1954". New York : Harper, 1955.

The report of Section V remains a cornerstone for ecumenical thinking on the issue of racial equality and justice. It deals with discrimination, effective participation in government, antisemitism and the need for a special WCC Department dealing with ethnic and racial conflicts and tensions.

1960   The Cottesloe Declaration. The Consultation Report is contained in "Mission in South Africa". Geneva : WCC, 1961.

A (multiracial) delegation of the WCC and South African member churches participated in a racial consultation at Cottesloe (Johannesburg). The common statement, with far reaching recommendations, was adopted with more than 80% of votes of the South African delegates. Black people's rights to own land, to equal work opportunities and education, and to participation in the government are stressed.

1961   "The New Delhi Report. The Third Assembly of the World Council of Churches 1961". London : SCM Press, 1962.

The withdrawal from the WCC of three Dutch Reformed Churches in South Africa after the Cottesloe Consultation was a reminder for Christians in the ecumenical movement of the difficulty in resolving the race problem. The New Delhi Assembly affirms the declaration of the Evanston Assembly and welcomes the establishment of the WCC Secretariat on Racial and Ethnic Relations.

1963   "Minutes and Reports of the Seventeenth Meeting of the Central Committee. Rochester, New York, 26 August - 2 September, 1963". Geneva : WCC, 1964.

Meeting at the time of the Civil Rights March led by Martin Luther King in Washington the WCC Central Committee adopted a statement on racial and ethnic tensions recognising that "the struggle is approaching its climax" and asking churches (particularly in the USA and South Africa) to intensify efforts for a peaceful solution of the race-problem.

1964   The National Council of Churches of Christ in the USA voted in February 1964 to ask the WCC assistance for a project in the Mississippi Delta area for direct relief for the needy, literacy training, reconciliation between racial groups, and community development. The WCC General Secretary issued a statement.

1964   "Christians and Race Relations in Southern Africa". Report on an Ecumenical Consultation held at Kitwe, Zambia, 25 May - 2 June, 1964. Geneva : WCC, Department on Church and Society, 1964.

This consultation, under the auspices of the WCC Church and Society Department, the South African Institute of Race Relations and the Mindolo Ecumenical Foundation, discussed the following issues : involvement of the churches, the trend from non-violence to violence, racial patterns in economic structures of society.

tion and use of banking deposit facilities and the continuation of banking relationships by the WCC.

1981   "Central Committee of the World Council of Churches. Minutes of the Thirty-Third Meeting, Dresden, FRG, 16-26 August 1981".

Recorded the thanks of the WCC to the Aboriginal people and their organizations, as well as to the Australian Council of Churches for the hospitality and for the help given to the WCC delegation. Agreed that the WCC investigate the possibility of delegates from the International Commission of Jurists, the UN Human Rights Commission and Amnesty International making similar visits to Australian Aboriginal communities.

1982   "Report of the Consultation on the Churches' Involvement in Southern Africa, Mindolo Ecumenical Centre, Kitwe, Zambia, 24-28 May, 1982".

The consultation, jointly sponsored by the All Africa Conference of Churches and PCR, made recommendations on : a) Theological Tasks; b) Relations with Liberation Movements; c) Education and Leadership Development; d) Action on Special Issues; e) Churches in South Africa and Namibia; f) Churches in the Region and the Rest of Africa; g) Task and Responsibility of Churches outside Africa. It issued a final report which outlined the priorities of liberation movements and the churches' cooperation with them.

1982   "Central Committee of the World Council of Churches. Minutes of the Thirty-Fourth Meeting, Geneva, 19-28 July, 1982".

Agreed to appeal to member churches to listen to and to learn from indigenous people struggling for their land rights, to commit significant financial and human resources to their struggle, to act as a sign to the wider community of the churches' commitment to justice for indigenous people, to urge their governments to ratify and implement all relevant United Nations and other intergovernmental instruments for the protection of the rights of indigenous people. Received with appreciation the report of the Mindolo consultation, urged the participation of liberation leaders in the Vancouver Assembly and giving the liberation of South Africa and Namibia the highest visibility at the Assembly.

1983   "Gathered for Life. Official Report of the VIth Assembly of the World Council of Churches, Vancouver, Canada, 24 July - 10 August, 1983". Ed. by David Gill. Geneva : WCC; Grand Rapids : W.B. Eerdmans, 1983.

Noted in Issue 6, "Struggling for Justice and Human Dignity", that racism is often aggravated by international system backed by powerful economic and military factors. Issued a Statement on Southern Africa which included fifteen recommendations. Issued a resolution on the rights of the Aboriginal peoples of Canada which urged the Federal and Provincial governments of that nation to recognize and enact Aboriginal title, Aboriginal rights and treaty rights in the Canadian Constitution in a manner and form acceptable to the Aboriginal peoples themselves.

1984   "Central Committee of the World Council of Churches. Minutes of the Thirty-Sixth Meeting, Geneva, 9-18 July, 1984".

Recalled the Vancouver Assembly Statement on Southern Africa; reaffirmed the WCC's longstanding commitment to take all appropriate steps to support the struggle for lasting justice and liberation in the region; emphasized that the Constitutional Proposals are fraudulent and racist because they do not provide for the real sharing of power and exclude blacks entirely from the political process; noted that the forced removals of people from the "blackspots" cause even greater hardship among the black population and tear families apart; expressed joy that churches inside South Africa have been critical of these developments and that there are significant manifestations of the unity and strength of the black people through new movements for justice and dignity.

1985   "Central Committee of the World Council of Churches. Minutes of the Thirty-Seventh Meeting, Buenos Aires, Argentina, 28 July - 8 August, 1985".

Noted the state of emergency in South Africa; re-emphasized economic pressure on the country; noted the failure of "constructive engagement"; reminded of the constant violence and oppression of the South African government in Namibia; stressed the hopeless future of the young generation under apartheid; called for renewed Christian concern and action; expressed continued admiration and support for the prophetic and courageous stand of the South African Council of Churches and the Council of Churches in Namibia; reiterated its support for the ongoing process of consultation and solidarity among the churches in Africa, in cooperation with the All Africa Conference of Churches.

ECUMENICAL STATEMENTS ON RACISM AND THE STRUGGLE AGAINST IT — SINCE 1948

STATEMENTS FROM THE FIRST ASSEMBLY OF THE WORLD COUNCIL OF CHURCHES AMSTERDAM (1948)

1. The Report of Section III — The Church and the Disorder of Society — "The Social Function of the Church" (Excerpt from Part V, p. 195)

... If the Church can overcome the national and social barriers which now divide it, it can help society to overcome those barriers. This is especially clear in the case of racial distinction. It is here that the Church has failed most lamentably, where it has reflected and then by its example sanctified the racial prejudice that is rampant in the world. And yet it is here that today its guidance concerning what God wills for it is especially clear. It knows that it must call society away from prejudice based upon race or colour and from the practices of discrimination and segregation as denials of justice and human dignity, but it cannot say a convincing word to society unless it takes steps to eliminate these practices from the Christian community, because they contradict all that it believes about God's love for all His children.

2. The Report of Section IV — The Church and the International Disorder — "The Observance of Human Rights and Fundamental Freedoms" Excerpts from Part IV, p. 221)

We are profoundly concerned by evidence from many parts of the world of flagrant violations of human rights. Both individuals and groups are subjected to persecution and discrimination and groups are subjected to persecution and discrimination on grounds of race, colour, religion, culture or political conviction. Against such actions, whether of governments, officials, or the general public, the churches must take a firm and vigorous stand, through local action, in cooperation with churches in other lands, and through international institutions of legal order. They must work for an ever wider and deeper understanding of what are the essential human rights if men are to be free to do the will of God.

3. From the Youth Report of Section III — The Church and the Disorder of Society — "The Task of the Church" (Excerpt from Part III)

The Church as a worshipping body is the community of people who have found oneness in Jesus Christ. We strongly affirm our conviction that the Body of Christ cannot be divided by racial class and other discriminations, and that any church or Christian group which upholds them in the name of Christ, is denying the very meaning of the Christian faith.

STATEMENT FROM THE SECOND ASSEMBLY OF THE WORLD COUNCIL OF CHURCHES EVANSTON (1954)

Report of Section V — Inter-Group Relations

The Church Amid Racial And Ethnic Tensions.

III **The Calling of the Church** (p. 153)

This is the calling of the Church with regard to race, to witness within itself to the Kingship of Christ and the unity of His people, in Him transcending all diversity. Jesus Christ in His incarnation and redemptive action restores this unity which from the beginning was God's design.

Their calling requires Christians to witness to the Kingship of Christ and the unity of all mankind, and to strive through social and political action to secure justice, freedom and peace for all as a foretaste of that Kingdom into which the faithful shall be gathered.

All Churches and Christians are involved, whether they recognize it or not, in the racial and ethnic tensions of the world. But it is in communities where segregation prevails that they face the plainest difficulties and the most challenging opportunities; for such segregation denies to those who are segregated their just and equal rights and results in deep injuries to the human spirit, suffered by offender and victim alike.

The great majority of Christian churches affiliated with the World Council have declared that physical separation within the Church on grounds of race is a denial of spiritual unity, and of the brotherhood of man. Yet such separation persists within these very churches, and we often seek to justify them on other grounds than race, because in our own hearts we know that separation solely on the grounds of race is abhorrent in the eyes of God.

We seek to justify such exclusion on the ground of difference of culture, or on the ground that a residential pattern of segregation necessitates it, or on the ground that the time is not yet ripe. We even say that we are willing to abandon all separations, but must retain them because so many others are unwilling to abandon them. We often make use of the unregenerateness of the world to excuse our own.

22

IV Repentance and Obedience (p. 154)

... The problems of race, difficult as they are, insoluble as they sometimes appear to be, provide for Christians an opportunity for obedience, and for a deeper understanding that bond and free, Jew and Gentile, Greek and Barbarian, people of every land and continent, are all one in Christ.

If Christian obedience leads to suffering, that is part of the price. For the Lord of all was in Gethsemane in an agony, and His sweat was as it were great drops of blood falling down to the ground; but He endured the cross, despising the shame, for the joy that was set before Him.

When we are given Christian insight the whole pattern of racial discrimination is seen as an unutterable offence against God to be endured no longer, so that the very stones cry out. In such moments we understand more fully the meaning of the Gospel, and the duty of both Church and Christian.

V The Task of the Churches (p. 155)

Racial and ethnic fears, hates, and prejudices are more than social problems with whose existence we must reckon; they are sins against God and His commandments that the Gospel alone can cure. To the Church has been committed the preaching of the Gospel; to proclaim "the healing of the nations" through Christ is verily her task. The Gospel has a power of its own, which manifests itself despite the shortcomings of the churches.

... The Church of Christ cannot approve of any law which discriminates on grounds of race, which restricts the opportunity of any person to acquire education to prepare himself for his vocation, to procure or to practise employment in his vocation, or in any other way curtails his exercise of the full rights and responsibilities of citizenship and of sharing in the responsibilities and duties of government. While it can find in the Bible no clear justification or condemnation of intermarriage but only a discussion of the duties of the faithful in marriage with partners of other religions, it cannot approve any law against racial or ethnic intermarriage, for Christian marriage involves primarily a union of two individuals before God which goes beyond the jurisdiction of the State or culture.

Resolution adopted by the Assembly (p. 158)

I   The Second Assembly of the World Council of Churches declares its conviction that any form of segregation based on race, colour, or ethnic origin is contrary to the Gospel, and is incompatible with the Christian doctrine of man and with the nature of the Church of Christ. The Assembly urges the churches within its membership to renounce all forms of segregation or discrimination and to work for their abolition within their own life and within society.

II   This Second Assembly of the World Council of Churches recognizes that one of the major problems of social justice in situations involving racial and ethnic tensions is that of securing for all the opportunities for the free exercise of responsible citizenship and for effective participation by way of franchise in both local and central government activity. It commends this matter to the attention of all Christian people for such action as, under God, they may be led to take in order to secure the solution of this problem.

IV The Second Assembly recommends to the Central Committee that, in consultation with the International Missionary Council, it make structural provision for an organization, preferably a department, giving assistance to the constituent churches in their efforts to bring the Gospel to bear more effectively upon relations between racial and ethnic groups. Such organization should provide leadership and assistance not only in (a) continuing study of the problems of inter-group relations, especially of racial and ethnic tensions; (b) exchanging information on the matter of racial and ethnic groups and on the positions and work of the churches; and (c) producing and distributing reports and educational materials to increase concern and understanding with regard to these matters in the constituency of the Council; but should also be the means whereby the various contributions of the rich cultural heritages of the groups within the Council's constituency may strengthen the life and witness of all the churches and of this Council as a whole.

STATEMENT FROM A CONSULTATION OF WCC MEMBER CHURCHES IN SOUTH AFRICA (Cottesloe 1960)

PART I (p. 29)

We have met as delegates from the member churches in South Africa of the World Council of Churches, together with representatives of the World Council itself, to seek under the guidance of the Holy Spirit to understand the complex problems of human relationships in this country, and to consult with one another on our common task and responsibility in the light of the Word of God.

PART II (p. 30)

1. We recognize that all racial groups who permanently inhabit our country are a part of our total population, and we regard them as indigenous. Members of all these groups have an equal right to make their contribution towards the enrichment of the life of their country and to share in the ensuing responsibilities, rewards and privileges.

2. The present tension in South Africa is the result of a long historical development and all groups bear responsibility for it. This must also be seen in relation to events in other parts of the world. The South African scene is radically affected by the decline of the power of the West and by the desire for self-determination among the peoples of the African continent.

3. The Church has a duty to bear witness to the hope which is in Christianity both to white South Africans in their uncertainty and the non-white South Africans in their frustration.

4. In a period of rapid social change the Church has a special responsibility for fearless witness within society.

5. The Church as the Body of Christ is a unity and within this unity the natural diversity among men is not annulled but sanctified.

6. No-one who believes in Jesus Christ may be excluded from any Church on the grounds of his colour or race. The spiritual unity among all men who are in Christ must find visible expression in acts of common worship and witness, and in fellowship and consultation on matters of common concern.

7. We regard with deep concern the revival in many areas of African society of heathen tribal customs incompatible with Christian beliefs and practice. We believe this reaction is partly the result of a deep sense of frustration and a loss of faith in Western civilization.

8. The whole Church must participate in the tremendous missionary tasks which has to be done in South Africa, and which demands a common strategy.

9. Our discussions have revealed that there is not sufficient consultation and communication between the various racial groups which make up our population. There is a special need that a more effective consultation between the government and leaders accepted by the non-white people of South Africa should be devised. The segregation of racial groups carried through without effective consultation and involving discrimination leads to hardship for members of the groups affected.

10. There are no Scriptural grounds for the prohibition of mixed marriages. The well-being of the community and pastoral responsibility require, however, that due consideration should be given to certain factors which may make such marriages inadvisable.

11. We call attention once again to the disintegrating effects of migrant labour on African life. No stable society is possible unless the cardinal importance of family life is recognized, and, from the Christian standpoint, it is imperative that the integrity of the family be safeguarded.

12. It is now widely recognized that the wages received by the vast majority of the non-white people oblige them to exist well below the generally accepted minimum standard for healthy living. Concerted action is required to remedy this grave situation.

13. The present system of job reservation must give way to a more equitable system of labour which safeguards the interests of all concerned.

14. Opportunities must be provided for the inhabitants of the Bantu areas to live in conformity with human dignity.

15. It is our conviction that the right to own land wherever he is domiciled, and to participate in the government of his country, is part of the dignity of the adult man, and for this reason a policy which permanently denies to non-white peoeple the right of collaboration in the government of the country of which they are citizens cannot be justified.

16. (a) It is our conviction that there can be no objection in principle to the direct representation of Coloured people in Parliament.

(b) We express the hope that consideration will be given to the application of this principle in the foreseeable future.

17. In so far as nationalism grows out of a desire for self-realization Christians should understand and respect it. The anger of nationalism is, however, that it may seek to fulfil its aim at the expense of the interests of others and that it can make the nation an absolute value which takes the place of God. The role of the Church must therefore be to help to direct national movements towards just and worthy ends.

STATEMENT FROM THE THIRD ASSEMBLY OF THE WORLD COUNCIL OF CHURCHES, NEW DELHI (1961)

... Where oppression, discrimination and segregation exist, the churches should identify themselves with the oppressed race in its struggle to achieve justice. Christians should be ready to lead in this struggle. The revolution is taking place whether we recognize it or not, and without Christian leadership it may be tragically perverted. The churches also have a duty to the oppressor in a ministry of education and reconciliation.

Racism and the consequent affronts to human dignity in the modern world often cause oppressed people to resort to violence when they have no other option. We urge all those in power to refrain from the use of violence and to avoid provoking it. Also we must say that the Gospel of Christ specifically urges that hate be met with love, and evil conquered with good. Therefore we call upon all Christians to encourage and support all efforts which seek through the non-violent way, to combat human indignities and to construct a community permeated by justice and reconciliation. The Church should seek to ensure that immigration laws are not based on race discrimination.

The Local Congregation

... It is not enough that local congregations should be racially inclusive in the formal sense. Members of minority groups are often hesitant about going into a Church dominated by another racial group. There is therefore a further task — the creation of a climate of warm acceptance of minority groups which may have different ways of worship, and other gifts, that will enrich the whole Church.

When communities are not involved in direct racial tensions, it is often because they segregate themselves by choice and so evade the problems of "intergroup living". Often they contain the very people who by their social position could do most for race relations.

The complacency of a secure and homogenous community may have to be disturbed by a Christian initiative in inviting people of different races into it.

Leadership in the Church

Dominations in their own structures must give a lead to ensure that there is no race discrimination in the Church. The churches are further called to utilize people of different races in positions of leadership, on the basis of merit only. Pastors should not be assigned only to churches of their own race and Christians should be prepared to accept a minister of another race. Missionary appointments, executive and administrative posts within the churches should be open to qualified persons regardless of race. Churches should give equal opportunity for training to all potential leaders and take special pains to foster the gifts of those less privileged. All Christian institutions should have open policies with respect to housing and employment.

Separate Development

All races, as indeed all persons, have their own unique contribution to make to the fellowship of human society, but we cannot agree that this is a reason for "separate development". On the contrary, it is only in community with others of diverse gifts that persons or communities can give of their best. The expression "separate but equal" is in concrete actuality a contradiction in terms.

ASSEMBLY RESOLUTIONS

On Racial and Ethnic Tensions (p. 187)

The Third Assembly of the World Council of Churches meeting at New Delhi, having considered the serious and far reaching implications of racial and ethnic tensions for the mission of the Church in the world, in the light of Christian unity, witness and service :

(1) Calls attention of the member churches to the mounting racial and ethnic tensions which accompany rapid social change and the struggle for social justice in many areas.

(2) Notes with gratitude :

  (a) The witness of churches and their members in difficult situations, struggling to uphold the unity of the Christian fellowship transcending racial and ethnic divisions;

  (b) The courage and sacrifice of individuals and groups, both Christians and non-Christians who, in spite of forces urging to violence, are giving leadership in the struggle for human rights in a spirit of forgiveness and non-violence;

  (c) Those churches, though divided by different approaches to the question of race relations, willing to meet with each other within the unity of the Christian faith, to talk to each other and to discover together the will of God for their common witness to Christ in society.

(3) Welcomes the establishment of the WCC Secretariat on Racial and Ethnic Relations and urges the member churches to give support to developing the programme of the Secretariat.

(4) Reminds all the churches of the declaration by the Evanston Assembly on Inter-group relations that "any form of segregation based on race, colour or ethnic origin is contrary to the Gospel, and is incompatible with the Christian doctrine of man with the nature of the Church of Christ", and urges them to act more resolutely than they have heretofore "to renounce all forms of segregation or discrimination and to work for their abolition within their own life and within society".

STATEMENT FROM MEETING OF THE WCC
CENTRAL COMMITTEE ROCHESTER, NEW YORK (1963)

(p. 142)

The movement to secure full human and civil rights for Negro citizens in the United States has now become a tide which cannot be turned back. Nor is it any longer a purely internal issue. It is rather an integral part of worldwide racial tension, and as such has become a matter of deep concern for Christians everywhere. The Central Committee pays tribute to all those in the United States, Negro, white and others, who have suffered in this cause. It commends those parishes, individuals and Christian organizations which are struggling to remove this blemish from the life of the nation. It laments that there are still white citizens desperately trying to perpetuate patterns of racial segregation in church and school, in housing and employment, and in public accommodation. In the centennial year of the Emancipation Proclamation and in the week of the unprecedented demonstration in Washington for civil rights, the Central Committee calls on the churches of the United States to intensify efforts to eliminate all forms of racial discrimination from every aspect of life in their country. The churches have much to do in order to bring their practice in race relations into accord with their policy. The time has come for them to work to get the international implications and ramifications of the crisis understood. The time has come for them to strive together to help remove every trace of discrimination from the national life. The time has come for them to redouble efforts to develop genuine communication between Negro and other citizens to fulfill the ministry of reconciliation.

The demand for racial and ethnic equality is being made in many places; and will continue until it is attained everywhere in full. We remind ourselves that the references to South Africa and the United States present a challenge to all our consciences, to do in our own countries, cities and churches all that we should for racial justice and Christian fellowship. The solution demanded requires radical change in long-established patterns of thought and action. Wherever fear of such change may exist, we must recall that when God is present, as surely He is in this matter, there is no need for fear. One further grave consequence of the struggle for racial equality is that it sets up barriers to open communication between individuals, between races, between governments, between organizations, and even between churches. But openness and free communication are indispensable to the attainment of the goal.

The promise of the Holy Spirit is the guarantee that these things are possible.

28

STATEMENT BY THE WCC GENERAL SECRETARY ON THE MISSISSIPPI DELTA PROJECT — GENEVA (1964)

The request which has come from the National Council of Churches (USA) to the World Council of Churches' Division of Inter-Church Aid, Refugee, and World Service, to list for worldwide support a comprehensive project in the Mississippi Delta represents a new and important departure in the realm of inter-church aid and ecumenical solidarity. Never before has the Division listed a project in the United States. Why then has this request been sent ? Not because the US churches are financially unable to meet the material and spiritual needs of the Mississippi Delta. Rather because they feel that they desire that their sister-churches in other countries should be involved in meeting this great need and they desire to profit by the experience of other Christians who have ministered in areas of great tension.

The Mississippi Delta is a symbol of resistance to full racial equality and the race problem is a world problem which the whole Christian world must help to solve. From the point of view of the ecumenical movement we are grateful for this action of the churches in the USA which gives evidence of their deep practical awareness of the truth that the ecumenical attitude is to be ready to receive as well as to give, which thus renders witness to the true meaning of inter-church aid.

STATEMENT FROM THE MINDOLO CONSULTATION ON CHRISTIAN PRACTICE AND DESIRABLE ACTION IN SOCIAL CHANGE AND RACE RELATIONS IN SOUTHERN AFRICA (1964)

A primary concern of our consultation has been to ask how we may recapture something of the autonomy, the dignity, and the integrity of the Church in the midst of the racially divided societies in Southern Africa. We have seen anew the need for a courageous ministry, dedicated leadership, a loyal laity and youth prepared to represent the communion of God's people among the peoples of Southern Africa. In reaction to white prejudice, many non-whites are developing a revolutionary attitude born of the realization that the white group which sets the patterns of society is oblivious to the deepest human aspirations of its underprivileged partners. The present social stratification seems to the Africans to deprive them of any Christian, as well as civic, responsibility towards society at large.

In this situation of racial tensions and sensitivity, the churches are particularly vulnerable if their leaders, indigenous and expatriate, clergy and laity, are not fully committed to the responsible autonomy, dignity and equality of all churches.

Urgency of the Situation (p. 12)

As the discussion proceeded, the urgency of the situation became increasingly clear to every member. The decisions by African States taken individually and collectively, the training of "freedom fighters" in different parts of Africa, the increased defence and military measures of the governments concerned, the strong determination of two opposing groups — one passionately determined to retain its present privileged position and the other just as passionately determined to alter it — all add up to a situation fraught with dangerous possibilities.

Although it is felt in some circles that the implementation of the Bantustan policy and the general economic development in South Africa has reduced tensions, there was general agreement among us that the situation has increased in gravity to such an extent that it has almost reached a point of no return. In spite of this, the impression remains that large numbers of people in Southern Africa are still ignorant of the factual situation or the issues at stake, while others live in a false complacency that the military power and measures of their governments will ensure prolonged peace and prosperity and the maintenance of the status quo.

The Trend from Non-Violence to Violence (p. 13)

The urgency of the situation in South Africa is further increased by the conviction of leading Africans that, as all peaceful measures tried by African political organizations over a period of many years to bring about an ordered change have proved abortive, only one avenue remains open — that of violence. On the other hand, it is precisely this conviction and possible resultant action which consolidates the white electorate, hardens its general attitude, and leads to ever-increasing measures which eventually precipitate the danger they wish to avoid. For many Christians involved in the struggle for a just solution, the question of possible violence as the only remaining alternative has become an urgent and ever-pressing one. Reports indicate that many are convinced that war has already begun. Although there is still a slender chance for a negotiated settlement in Southern Rhodesia, already a similar polarization of social attitudes has taken place there. It is feared that any outbreak of racial violence on a large scale in any part of Southern Africa may seriously affect the situation in all other areas and adversely influence the possibility of peaceful negotiation and solution.

Many African leaders maintain that violence has never been desired or sought if any other mode of effective negotiation could be established or remained open. The Consultation feared that if the urgency of the situation is not recognized, negotiation established, and further effective measures taken, violence will increase. Every inhabitant of Southern Africa bears a heavy responsibility to do everything in his power to prevent this.

Racial Patterns in Economic Life : The Challenge to Christians (p. 19)

There can and should be no doubt of the Christian concern for the injustices in the dual pattern of economic life in Southern Africa. Indeed, in view of the involvement of many lay Christians in the struggle for economic justice in countries of Southern Africa, the Church must ask whether it had done enough to support them. It must not cease to remind those in authority of the moral judgments upon the many features of the dual economic system which are repugnant to Christian conscience. These include :

30

a) The great inequalities of wealth and income between racial groups, and the social conflicts and sense of injustice which they engender.

b) The selfish possession by a minority racial group of great economic power over the majority racial group.

c) The frustration of the sense of Christian vocation which comes from the inability of Christians of a particular race to realize their abilities and capacities as persons, due to arbitrary restrictions and restraints upon their economic activity. The fact that these restrictions are imposed by other Christians who are in authority, increases the moral responsibility of the Church.

The victims of these economic injustices are looking to the Church largely in vain, to secure relief for their grievances. There is already much disillusionment with Christianity and many are looking elsewhere for relief. Churches have to prepare themselves to speak out against specific injustices in economic life; they must set an example in their own institutional life and by their sacrificial witness and action for man in society; and they must support every movement leading to the improvement of economic conditions for the African.

The Call to Churches and Christians (p. 14)

The Commission was convinced that we have no right to speak to anybody else unless we first speak to ourselves and our fellow-Christians. The Church of Christ and all its members must come to a sincere recognition and confession of their guilt in a situation for which they have long been responsible, a guilt which we must bear with, and on behalf of, the whole community. It includes the guilt of sinful silence when there was urgent need to speak both in prophecy and in reconciliation, of lack of identification with the suffering and the oppressed, of indifference and unwillingness to become involved, of lack or real fellowship among Christians, and of neglect of duty in the education of the laity through proclamation and instruction. There is no renewal possible without confession, supplication, intercession, and identification. Once this is understood and accepted, many as yet unexploited avenues of witness, service and reconciliation will open to all Christians.

If unavoidable violence erupts, all Christians should use their full influence to limit it to the point at which there can be negotiation and settlement as early as possible. This is the time when Christian goodwill should lead to reconciliation, and thus lay the foundations of a new society.

WORLD CONFERENCE ON CHURCH AND SOCIETY — "CHRISTIANS IN THE TECHNICAL AND SOCIAL REVOLUTIONS OF OUR TIME". GENEVA, 1966

SECTION IV — MAN AND COMMUNITY IN CHANGING SOCIETIES (pp. 160-161)

25. In dealing with racial and ethnic problem, Christian churches must be fully aware of the political and economic structures of society and see the problems in their contexts. That is to say, socialist countries, capitalist countries, and countries with mixed economies are bound to present different contexts within which to view the racial and ethnic problems. However, basic human rights as seen from a Christian perspective, must not be compromised under any circumstances in any manner. Otherwise Christian faith fails to provide that unity of mankind which transcends political and economic factors.

26. Since the people who control the social, economic and political structures are also members of the dominant racial group, and have so far failed to ensure equal opportunity for members of minority or subordinated racial groups, our society remains racially divided and even stratified, reinforcing and perpetuating discriminating modes of racist thinking and behaviour.

27. In national and local societies of multi-ethnic composition, similar tensions exist between dominant ethnic groups and minority or subordinate ethnic groups. Ethnocentrism, whether based on racial, ethnic or tribal distinction, remains a dangerous stumbling block in the development of human community on the national and supranational level.

28. There are many instances of ethnocentrism within the church preventing the wholesome growth of national churches and the unity of Christian people. No continent, no nation, and few organized churches are without this problem.

SECTION V — CONCLUSIONS AND RECOMMENDATIONS (pp. 175-176)

Race Relations

84. In terms of general principles and guidelines for Christian action in dealing with the race issue, a great deal has been said clearly and repeatedly, from the standpoint of Christian moral theology and social ethics, by successive conferences and consultations of the WCC, and by its related agencies more particularly by the Evanston and New Delhi Assemblies. This Conference reaffirms both the guiding principles and the mandates contained in the Evanston and New Delhi statements on race relations. "...The Assembly urges the Church within its membership to renounce all forms of segregation or discrimination and to work for their abolition within their own life and within society." In face of the explosive situation, described earlier, we urge Christians and churches everywhere :

85. — to oppose, openly and actively, the perpetuation of the myth of racial superiority as it finds expression in social conditions and human behaviour as well as in laws and social structures.

86. — to engage in the common task of changing the structure of society through legislation, social planning, and corporate action, and to mobilize all its resources to ensure the full and equal participation of all racial and ethnic groups in the corporate life of a pluralistic society.

87. — to recognize, support, and share the individual and collective interests of people who are disadvantaged by their race and ethnic origin, so that they may gain the basic human, political, and economic rights enjoyed by the others in a pluralistic society.

88. — to make organized efforts to eradicate from the Church and Christian community all forms of discrimination based on race, colour or ethnic origin in the selection of persons for church leadership, admission to the membership of congregations, and in adapting social and cultural values and traditions to the present.

89. — to use the powers inherent in its administrative structure, such as those that come from the investment of its resources or from the influence of its means of communication, to correct racial malpractice in society as well as within the Church itself.

92. On the international scene, the Rhodesian situation is deplorable. This Conference regrets that successive British governments from 1951 onwards have been unable to secure a solution of the Rhodesian problem based upon majority rule. Satisfactory negotiations have not been held with African nationalist leaders, some of whom are unjustly detained. The WCC, the British Council of Churches and Rhodesian Council of Churches, and the overwhelming majority of world opinion have condemned the Smith regime, and the British government has repeatedly declared that it is illegal. We identify ourselves with the African nationals of Rhodesia in their quest for majority rule. Since to date the British government by itself has failed to bring about a just solution of the Rhodesian problem, this Conference recommends that the entire Rhodesian situation be referred to the United Nations.

SECTION III — THEOLOGICAL ISSUES IN RACIAL AND ETHNIC RELATIONS (pp. 204-205)

34. At this moment of history, the white race dominates the world economically and politically. This domination prevents the development of authentic human community both in nations and on an international level. Christians should be passionately concerned that this pattern of domination be broken down, in order that a more truly human society may be built. Christian theology has the responsibility to see this situation in historical perspective and to discern the need to destroy this idolatrous structure in order that God's purposes in history may be advanced.

35. Reconciliation in this context cannot be mere sentimental harmonizing of conflicting groups. It demands sacrifice. It demands identification with the oppressed. It demands determination to break down the unjust pattern. It should restore the dignity of the oppressed. Changes in personal attitudes and reconciliation of individual are of fundamental importance, but nothing less than structural change can create a pattern of justice in which the dignity and freedom of all will be assured.

36. It is not enough for churches and groups to condemn the sin of racial arrogance and oppression. The struggle for radical change in structures will inevitably bring suffering

and will demand costly and bitter engagement. For Christians to stand aloof from this struggle is to be disobedient to the call of God in history. The meaning of the Cross for our time can be nothing less than this.

STATEMENT FROM THE FOURTH ASSEMBLY OF THE WORLD COUNCIL OF CHURCHES UPPSALA (1968)

REPORT OF SECTION IV —
TOWARDS JUSTICE AND PEACE IN INTERNATIONAL AFFAIRS

Race Relations (pp. 65-66)

27. Contemporary racism robs all human rights of their meaning, and is an imminent danger to world peace. The crucial nature of the present situation is emphasized by the official policies of certain governments, racial violence in many countries, and the racial component in the gap between rich and poor nations. Only immediate action directed to root causes can avoid widespread violence or war.

28. Racism is a blatant denial of the Christian faith. (1) It denies the effectiveness of the reconciling work of Jesus Christ, through whose love all human diversities lose their divisive significance; (2) it denies our common humanity in creation and our belief that all men are made in God's image; (3) it falsely asserts that we find our significance in terms of racial identity rather than in Jesus Christ.

a) Racism is linked with economic, and political exploitation. The churches must be actively concerned for the economic and political well-being of exploited groups so that their statements and actions may be relevant. In order that victims of racism may regain a sense of their own worth and be enabled to determine their own future, the churches must make economic and educational resources available to underprivileged groups for their development to full participation in the social and economic life of their communities. They should also withdraw investments from institutions that perpetuate racism. They must also urge that similar assistance be given from both the public and private sectors. Such economic help is an essential compensatory measure to counteract and overcome the present systematic exclusion of victims of racism from the main stream of economic life. The churches must also work for the change of those political processes which prevent the victims of racism from participating fully in the civic and governmental structures of their countries.

b) Racism employs fallacious generalizations and distortions to sustain its existence, and these result in personal denigration, segregation and other forms of isolation. The churches must eradicate all forms of racism from their own life. That many have not done so, particularly where institutional racism assumes subtle forms, is a scandal. The churches must also fight to secure legislation to eliminate racism. This will involve new approaches in education and the mass media, so that false value-judgements can be eliminated and the true grounds of human dignity made evident to all mankind.

c) Racism produces counter-racism as a defensive measure for human survival. It also perpetuates itself from generation to generation. The Church must break this vicious spiral. It must confront individuals who hold racial prejudices with the truth about our common humanity and emphasize the personal worth of all men. It must demonstrate that the grace of God is sufficient to reconcile and unite all members of the human race.

d) The Secretariat of Race Relations of the World Council of Churches needs to be strengthened to help the churches embark on a vigorous campaign against racism.

Recommendations for Post-Assembly Programme (pp. 241-242)

The Elimination of Racism — A Programme of Study and Action

7. The World Council of Churches in numerous ecumenical statements since 1948 has recognized the increasing urgency for the Christian Church to participate actively in the struggle for racial equality, dignity and self-respect and has noted that this struggle is rapidly reaching a climax. The ominous events which have occurred since New Delhi 1961, oblige us to promote new efforts to eliminate racism.

8. By racism we mean ethnocentric *pride* in one's own racial group and preference for the distinctive characteristics of that group; belief that these characteristics are fundamentally biological in nature and are thus transmitted to succeeding generations; strong negative feelings towards other groups who do not share these characteristics coupled with the thrust to discriminate against and exclude the outgroup from full participation in the life of the community.

9. By *white racism* we mean the conscious or unconscious belief in the inherent superiority of persons of European ancestry (particularly those of Northern European origin), which entitles all white peoples to a position of dominance and privilege, coupled with the belief in the innate inferiority of all darker peoples, especially those of African ancestry, which justifies their subordination and exploitation. By focussing upon white racism, we are not unaware of other forms of ethnocentrism which produce inter-ethnic and inter-tribal tensions and conflicts throughout the world today.

10. We believe, however, that white racism has special historical significance because its roots lie in powerful, highly developed countries, the stability of which is crucial to any hope for international peace and development. The racial crisis in these countries is to be taken as seriously as the threat of nuclear war. The revolt against racism is one of the most inflammatory elements of the social revolution now sweeping the earth; it is fought at the level of mankind's deepest and most vulnerable emotions — the universal passion for human dignity. The threatened internal chaos of those countries in which racial conflict is most intense has immediate worldwide impact, for racism under attack tends to generate and to spread counter-racism. We submit that this crisis will grow worse unless we understand the historical phenomenon of white racism, what has distinguished it from other forms of intergroup conflict, and what must be done to resolve the crisis on the basis of racial justice.

11. It is urged that the World Council of Churches undertake a crash programme to guide the Council and the member churches in the urgent matter of racism. This programme would involve :

1) the development of comprehensive and up-to-date reports on the racial situation in various regions of the world. The prototype for this might well be the comprehensive PEP (Political and Economic Planning) report from the United Kingdom. Immediate studies are needed from Southern Africa, USA and Australia;

2) consultations on racism on a regional and international level;

3) creation of a consultant service to make available the counsel of experts to various secular and church agencies;

4) relating the view and experience of the Church to various international agencies, especially the United Nations;

5) research on the areas of potential crisis and alerting the churches and secular agencies in helping to prevent the growth of tension arising from racism;

6) action-coalition projects, particularly for developing models for action (e.g., in some of the joint action for mission projects);

7) mass educational materials on racial issues;

8) establishing within the General Secretariat a coordinated secretariat on the elimination of racism, and the appointment of an ecumenical commission to supervise this programme.

STATEMENT FROM THE WCC SPONSORED CONSULTATION ON RACISM NOTTING HILL, LONDON, MAY 19-24, 1969

Vincent, John. The Race Race, London : SCM, 1970, pp. 97-98

... More than once the Consultation itself was exposed to the pervasiveness of stereotypes, paternalism and, in the final result, attitudes of racial superiority that have developed over centuries. The churches reflect the world.

The identification of the churches with the *status quo* means today, as before that it has remained, in effect, part of the racial problem and not a means of eliminating it.

If the churches are to have any relevance in these critical times, it is imperative that they no longer concentrate their attention on the individual actions of individual Christians who are fighting racism. To the majority of Christians, the Church is a community, a group — perhaps even a movement — and it is therefore necessary that issues of racism be addressed by a group. Individual commitment is commendable — but not enough...

... It has become clear in the week's study and dialogue that racism is in large part an outgrowth of the struggle for power that afflicts all men. Racist ideologies and propaganda are developed and disseminated as tools in economic, political and military struggles for power. Once developed they have a life of their own, finding a place in the traditions and culture of a people, unless stringent and continuous effort is made to exercise them.

A second fact that has become clear is that the Church is not using the weapons it possesses to eradicate racism itself — even within its own institution. But the Church is charged with a ministry of reconciliation. And if it is to take that ministry seriously, then it must attack racism significantly — at its origin, as well as in its symptoms. Therefore, the Church must be willing to be not only an institution of love but also an institution of action, making inputs into societies to help effect a new balance of power that renders racism impotent. The Church must come to realize that in our institutionalized world the closest approximation to love possible, is justice.

To that end, the Consultation calls upon the World Council of Churches to take the following steps :

1. that the World Council of Churches and its members churches begin applying economic sanctions against corporations and institutions which practise blatant racism;

2. that the World Council of Churches and its member churches use every means available to influence governments in following a similar practice of economic sanctions to promote justice;

3. that the World Council of Churches and its members churches do support and encourage the principle of "reparations" to exploited peoples and countries (recognizing the churches' own involvement in such exploitation and hence, reparation) to the end of producing a more favourable balance of economic power throughout the world;

4. that the World Council of Churches should establish a unit with adequate resources to deal with the eradication of racism;

5. to circulate among member churches the UNESCO Report as background material to enable Christians to understand why the Church and church-related institutions must enter into the struggle against racism in areas of power;

6. that the World Council of Churches, through the initiative of its reorganized Commission of the Churches on International Affairs serves as the co-ordinating centre for the implementation of multiple strategies for the struggle against racism in Southern Africa by the churches;

7. that all else failing, the Church and churches support resistance movements, including revolutions, which are aimed at the elimination of political or economic tyranny which makes racism possible.

STATEMENT FROM THE CENTRAL COMMITTEE
CANTERBURY (1969)

PLAN FOR AN ECUMENICAL PROGRAMME TO COMBAT RACISM
(pp. 270-275) (as adopted by Central Committee)

II RECOMMENDATION REGARDING AN ECUMENICAL PROGRAMME TO COMBAT RACISM

Since its inception, the WCC consistently denounced the sin of racism. The issue is not new to us. But today it arises with a new and terrifying urgency. The WCC has offered a strong lead in the past, but its studies and statements generally have evoked neither adequate awareness nor effective action. Further, recent study and dialogue have served to open up dimensions and implications of the problem never before realized. Thus the struggle against racism as it rapidly intensifies is now confronting the churches with a challenge to deeper understanding, fresh commitment and costly redemptive action.

The Consultation recommended to the WCC and its member churches lines of action for an ecumenical programme to combat racism. However, more important than any recommendation, it pleaded for a profound and renewed commitment from the churches — and specifically from the World Council of Churches — to offer a convincing moral lead in the face of this great and growing crisis of our times.

To make the commitment quite concrete in the life of the World Council of Churches, the following prospectus is proposed for adoption :

The Scope and Focus of a New Ecumenical Programme to Combat Racism

Racism is not an unalterable feature of human life. Like slavery and other social manifestations of man's sin, it can and must be eliminated. In the light of the Gospel and in accordance with its principles and methods, Christians must be involved in this struggle and, wherever possible, in association with all people of goodwill.

Racism today is not confined to certain countries or continents. It is a world problem. White racism is not its only form. It is recognized that at this moment in some parts of the world, like Asia and Africa other forms of racism and ethnocentrism provide the most crucial problems. There is a strong element of racism in current forms of anti-semitism as well as in the discrimination against the lower castes in India.

It is the coincidence, however, of an accumulation of wealth and power in the hands of the white peoples, following upon their historical and economic progress during the past 400 years, which is the reason for a focus on the various forms of white racism in the different parts of the world. People of different colour suffer from this racism in all continents. Among situations are those of the Aborigines in Australia, the Maoris in New Zealand, the black majorities of Southern Africa, the Indians, Afro-Americans, and Hispano-Americans in the USA, the Indians and Eskimos in Canada, the Indians in various Latin American countries, the coloured immigrants and students in the UK and continental Europe (this is by no means an exhaustive list).

There was a period when "colonialism" was the main feature of white racism. Some areas still suffer in this way. While many formerly colonial peoples have become independent, they still suffer from the aftermath of "colonialism", part of which is the struggle for power between communities and tribes.

It is further recognized that the fight against racism in all its forms must be set within the context of the struggle for world community, including world development.

Rationale for an Ecumenical Programme to Combat Racism

Growing tensions and conflicts between the races demand urgent action; time is running out. The pervasiveness, persistence and viciousness of racism has challenged many Christians. But a sense of the impotence of the churches to achieve reconciliation has immobilized many others. Many have even despaired.

We have sadly to recognize that in spite of the battle that has been fought against racism by churches, mission agencies and councils of churches, often with heroic personal sacrifice, racism is now a worse menace than ever. We have also sadly to confess that churches have participated in racial discrimination. Many religious institutions of the white northern world have benefited from racially exploitative economic systems. Many church members are unaware of the facts of racism and of the involvement of their religious and secular institutions in its perpetuation. Lacking information about institutionalized racism and about the possibility of developing sophisticated strategies to secure racial justice, Christians often engage in irrelevant and timid efforts to improve race relations — too little and too late.

In our ecumenical fellowship there are churches from all parts of the world, some of which have benefited and some of which have suffered from these racially exploitative economic systems. What is needed is an ecumenical act of solidarity which would help to stem the deterioration in race relations. To do this, our action must cost something and must be affirmative, visible and capable of emulation.

The issue of reparations has been raised by some groups in the USA and at the WCC Consultation at Notting Hill. It cannot therefore be avoided. Many of the churches which are confronted by this demand belong to our ecumenical fellowship, and are called upon to make a meaningful response to this issue. The concept of reparations, however, is inadequate, for it seeks simply to apportion guilt for the past and highlights a method of action which leaves out of account the need for acts of compassion, brotherhood and community which go beyond any financial payment. The Gospel speaks to us of the cost of reconciliation both to those who have suffered and those who have inflicted suffering.

We call upon the churches to move beyond charity, grants and traditional programming to relevant and sacrificial action leading to new relationships of dignity and justice among all men and to become agents for the radical reconstruction of society. There can be no justice in our world without a transfer of economic resources to undergird the redistribution of political power and to make cultural self-determination meaningful. In this transfer of resources a corporate act by the ecumenical fellowship of churches can provide a significant moral lead.

Call to Member Churches for Self-Examination and Release of Resources

We call upon churches to confess their involvement in the perpetuation of racism. Churches should make an analysis of their financial situation in order to determine the degree to which their financial practices, domestic and international, contribute to the support of racially oppressive governments, discriminatory industries and inhuman working conditions. The impact will be greater if this is an ecumenical act.

The forces seeking to liberate non-white peoples from the oppressive yoke of white racism have appropriately demanded the participation of religious institutions in restoring wealth and power to people. We urge churches to make land available free or at low cost to racially oppressed groups for community and economic development. Churches which have benefited from racially exploitative economic systems should immediately allocate a significant portion of their total resources, without employing paternalistic mechanisms of control, to organizations of the racially oppressed or organizations supporting victims of racial injustice.

Outline of a Five-Year Programme of the World Council of Churches

Clearly a determined attack on racism must come as a commitment of the WCC and its divisions and departments and will involve :

1. Teams of inquiry focusing on selected areas in Latin America, North America, Asia, Australasia and the Pacific, Europe, Southern Africa, etc., to express ecumenical concern and to assist in formulating guidelines for ecumenical understanding and action;

2. Consultation on selected issues which obstruct common action in achieving racial justice, e.g. : the problem of sharing economic and political power, including the demand for "reparations" which has been made in a number of quarters, and other proposals for overcoming the economic burden of historic and contemporary racism; the meaning of racial identity; anti-semitism; inter-marriage;

3. Providing more opportunity for confrontation between those holding different positions on the meaning of racial justice and those advocating different methods for attaining it;

4. Examination of all the means available for promoting political actions towards the bringing about of racial justice, including economic sanctions, both on the part of the member churches and of governments;

5. Assisting the member churches in developing strategies for combatting racial injustice;

6. Examination of the ways in which the churches can stand for the rights of the victims of racism and meet their needs;

7. Examination of the programmes, budgets and structures of the World Council of Churches with a view to increasing support of efforts for racial justice;

8. Collection and circulation of the best analyses on racism — including theological analyses — and other data helpful to the churches for the information and education of their members;

9. Encouraging member churches and national and regional Councils of Churches to make the problem of racism within their own area a priority concern in their programmes.

Our struggle is not against flesh and blood. It is against the principalities, against the powers of evil, against the deeply entrenched demonic forces of racial prejudice and hatred that we must battle. Ours is a task of exorcism. The demons operate through our social, economic and political structures. But the root of the problem is as deep as human sin, and only God's love and man's dedicated response can eradicate it.

The World Council's programme is but part of that response. It is God's love and not the hatred of man that must ultimately triumph. By God's love, by the power of His Spirit, some day, soon, we shall overcome.

STATEMENT FROM THE WCC EXECUTIVE COMMITTEE ARNOLDSHAIN (FRG) (1970)

RECOMMENDATIONS BY THE INTERNATIONAL ADVISORY COMMITTEE FOR THE PROGRAMME TO COMBAT RACISM REGARDING SPECIAL FUND AS ADOPTED BY WCC EXECUTIVE COMMITTEE (pp. 53-54)

The International Advisory Committee recommends that the Special Fund shall be allocated in accordance with the following criteria :

1. The proceeds of the Fund shall be used to support organizations that combat racism, rather than welfare organizations that alleviate the effects of racism, which would normally be eligible for support of other units of the World Council of Churches.

2. (a) The focus of the grants should be on raising the level of awareness and on strengthening the organizational capability of racially oppressed people.

   (b) In addition we recognize the need to support organizations that align themselves with the victims of racial injustice and pursue the same objectives.

While these grants are made without control of the manner in which they are spent, they are at the same time a commitment of the Programme to Combat Racism to the causes the organizations themselves are fighting for.

3. (a) The situation in Southern Africa is recognized as a priority due to the overt and intensive nature of white racism and the increasing awareness on the part of the oppressed in their struggle for liberation.

   (b) In the selection of other areas we have taken account of those places where the struggle is most intensive and where a grant might make a substantial contribution to the process of liberation particularly where racial groups are in imminent danger of being physically or culturally exterminated.

   (c) In considering applications from organizations in countries of white and affluent majorities we have taken note only of those cases where political involvement precludes help from other sources.

4. Grants should be made with due regard to where they can have the maximum effect; token grants should not be made unless there is a possibility of their eliciting a substantial response from other organizations.

STATEMENT FROM THE CENTRAL COMMITTEE
ADDIS ABABA (1971)

(pp. 54-57)

A. 1. The Central Committee has carefully considered the various reactions to the decision of the Executive Committee at Arnoldshain and is of the opinion that these decisions were in accord with the Programme to Combat Racism agreed upon by the Central Committee at Canterbury and believes that further action should be taken along the lines indicated in the Report on the Programme to Combat Racism and the Programme and Research Budget 1971.

   2. It believes that the churches must always stand for the liberation of the oppressed and of victims of violent measures which deny basic human rights. It calls attention to the fact that violence is in many cases inherent in the maintenance of the status quo. Nevertheless, the WCC does not and cannot identify itself completely with any political movement, nor does it pass judgement on those victims of racism who are driven to violence as the only way left to them to redress grievances and so open the way for a new and more just social order.

   3. It notes that the question of violence cannot be fully discussed or resolved in the context of racial issues and requests that a study be undertaken under WCC auspices on violent and non-violent methods of social change in view of the growing concern about this issue among Christians in every part of the world.

   4. It requests the staff to study ways and means to prevent the use of violence by those sustaining the status quo when confronted by non-violent actions and demonstrations.

B. 1. The Central Committee urges the member churches to support fully the Programme to Combat Racism as presented to this meeting of the Central Committee.

2. The Central Committee initiates a new appeal to the member churches in support of the original minimum Special Fund appeal of US dollars 500,000 established at Canterbury. The Central Committee notes with appreciation that the Executive Committee has received assurance from all organizations which appealed up to the present for grants from the Special Fund that they will not use the grants received for military purposes but for activities in harmony with purposes of the WCC and its divisions. The Central Committee requests the PCR to bring special projects and programmes to the attention of the member churches for their support.

3. The Central Committee urges the member churches to support the 1971 United Nations International Year for Action to Combat Racism and Racial Discrimination in appropriate manner including :

    a) working to secure the support of national governments of the 1971 UN International Year for Action to Combat Racism and national governmental approval of the International Convention on the Elimination of all forms of Racism, the Convention on the Prevention of the Crime of Genocide, the International Convention on Human Rights, etc.;

    b) initiating an ecumenical programme which will include whenever possible the participation and support of other Christians and non-Christian bodies in developing appropriate national and local programmes for action in support of the UN International Year.

4. The Central Committee urges the member churches to make the elimination of racism and racial discrimination a primary concern and to initiate immediately a national ecumenical and/or denominational programme to combat racism which will include the following :

    a) development of a programme which will make full use of the education and communication resources within the churches to educate, inform, interpret to and involve the clergy and laity of the church in action programmes to eliminate racism and racial discrimination within church and society;

    b) make the elimination of racism and racial discrimination a primary educational task of the church. This will involve (1) making a thorough review of existing parish education materials and programmes to eliminate overt or covert racist content and (2) a new creative effort to develop parish education materials and programmes designed to contribute toward the elimination of racism and racial discrimination and to develop the conscientization of children, youth and adults.

5. The Central Committee urges the WCC staff and committees and member churches to begin an immediate study and analysis of their involvement in the support and perpetuation of racism in the following areas :

a) investment policies and practices;

b) employment training and promotion schedules;

c) the ownership, management and control of property;

d) the ownership, management and control of church and church-related institutions;

and that the results of this study and analysis be reported to the Central Committee through the PCR at its next meeting. Where this has already been done, the results of this study and analysis should be updated and included in the report.

6. The Central Committee urges the member churches themselves or through their respective national councils to :

a) investigate and analyse the military, political, industrial and financial systems of their countries to discover and identify the involvement and support provided by these systems in the perpetuation of racism and racial discrimination in the domestic and in the foreign policies of their countries and coordinate their findings through the Programme to Combat Racism;

b) develop individually or in cooperation with other churches strategies and action programmes designed to redirect these systems to contribute to the elimination of racism and racial discrimination, and to promote racial justice, and

c) develop in cooperation with the Programme to Combat Racism and between themselves joint strategy and planning to secure and maintain full and mutual cooperation and support in their efforts to eliminate racism and racial discrimination in church and society.

To this end the Central Committee welcomes the invitation of South African churches for consultation on joint strategy and action.

STATEMENT FROM THE CENTRAL COMMITTEE UTRECHT (1972)

Special Fund (pp. 27-29)

... It was unanimously *agreed* that the Central Committee :

decides to extend the Special Fund to Combat Racism from US dollars 500,000 to a minimum of US dollars 1 million;

appeals to the member churches, groups and individuals to support the Fund as a minimum indication of their commitment to the objectives of the Programme to Combat Racism;

suggests that the background document be circulated to all member churches with the communication renewing the appeal.

Rhodesia. On the recommendation of Policy Reference Committee II, it was *agreed* that the Central Committee :

supports the call of the African National Council in Rhodesia for a national convention leading to a Constitutional Conference in order to achieve a "just, honourable and democratic settlement" in Rhodesia;

endorses the action of the Executive Committee in Auckland urging the government of the United Kingdom to exercise its continuing responsibility until full political rights for all the peoples of Rhodesia are achieved;

strongly confirms the action of the Executive Committee in Auckland urging WCC member churches in all countries to press upon their governments the necessity to make more effective economic sanctions and to apply the strongest political pressures against the present Rhodesian regime so long as the racially discriminatory system prevails there;

commends the action of the British Council of Churches in urging the government of the United Kingdom effectively to maintain sanctions against Rhodesia and to continue to withhold recognition from the illegal government in the colony;

deplores the decision of the United States of America to violate the United Nations' mandatory sanctions against Rhodesia by lifting the embargo on the importation of chrome from Rhodesia and calls upon the government of the United States to reconsider this decision as a matter of urgency; and

appeals to all member churches to cooperate with the CCIA and the PCR in a vigorous programme to sensitize trade unions and other influential sectors of public opinion to act in favour of intensifying United Nations' sanctions against Rhodesia.

Investments in Southern Africa. (p. 28) The Policy Reference Committee II had considered proposals concerning investments in Southern Africa submitted by the Unit Committee, together with a relevant background document approved by the PCR Executive Committee. After discussion of these proposals the Committee had subsequently held a joint meeting with the Finance Committee and though this meeting had resulted in the adoption of some amendments to the text of the proposals now before the Central Committee it had not been possible to reach complete agreement.

The adoption of the Policy Reference Committee's proposals were moved as follows :

The World Council of Churches, in accordance with its own commitment to combat racism, considering that the effect of foreign investments in Southern Africa is to strengthen the white minority regimes in their oppression of the majority of the people of this region, and implementing the policy as commended by the Uppsala Assembly (1968) that investments in "institutions that perpetuate racism" should be terminated :

i) *instructs* its Finance Committee and its Director of Finance to sell forthwith existing holdings and to make no investments after this date in corporations which, according to information available to the Finance Committee and the Director of Finance, are directly involved in investment in or trade with any of the following countries : South Africa, Namibia, Zimbabwe, Angola, Mozambique and Guinee-Bissao; and to deposit none of its funds in banks which maintain direct banking operations in those countries;

ii) *urges* all members churches, Christians agencies and individual Christians outside Southern Africa to use all their influence, including stockholder action and disinvestment, to press corporations to withdraw investments from and cease trading with these countries.

In the context of the multiple strategies recommended at Addis Ababa, the Central Committee is aware of and appreciates proposals to achieve racial justice in Southern Africa through reform (e.g. : the preliminary statement by the Evangelical Church in Germany). The Central Committee is nevertheless convinced that the policy of withdrawal already commended by the Uppsala Assembly needs to be implemented now.

STATEMENT FROM THE EXECUTIVE COMMITTEE
BAD-SAAROW (DDR) (1974)

South Africa and Namibia (p. 16)

... The Committee considered the growing repression of individuals and groups who are working for racial justice in South Africa. The following statement was ADOPTED for publication :

The Executive Committee of the World Council of Churches

— expresses alarm at the increasingly repressive measures being taken by the government of the Republic of South Africa, such as activities of its Schlebusch Commission, its lengthening list of banned persons, and the widespread persecution of dissenting voices of South Africans and Namibians (whose country South Africa illegally occupies);

— reaffirms the World Council's support for all persons and groups in those countries who are bearing courageous witness to the Christian vision of justice and reconciliation.

STATEMENT FROM THE CENTRAL COMMITTEE
WEST-BERLIN (1974)

Continuation of PCR (pp. 36-38)

1. After full examination of the issues raised, the Central Committee resolves to con-
    tinue the Programme to Combat Racism as an ongoing programme of the WCC,
    reaffirming the lines of policy as laid down in the Minutes of the Central Commit-
    tees at Canterbury (1969), Addis Ababa (1971) and Utrecht (1972), and re-appointing
    the present Commission.

Bishop Oliver Tomkins proposed as an amendment that after the words "the WCC"
there be inserted the words : "to be reviewed, together with all other programmes, at the
Fifth Assembly. The Central Committee reaffirms the lines of policy..."

After considerable discussion, the amendment was put to the vote and lost, and resolution (1) was carried.

2. The Central Committee resolves to continue to make grants from the Special Fund
    to movements of the racially oppressed and to organizations supporting the victims
    of racial injustice, with a minimum target of US dollars 300,000 to be raised and
    distributed each year.

3. The Central Committee resolves that increased consultation with the churches of the
    regions and regional participation in cooperation with racially oppressed groups be
    further encouraged and that guidelines for future work of the Programme be sub-
    mitted for discussion at the Fifth Assembly in 1975. It further requests that the PCR
    study the need for multiple strategies in combatting racism and report to the
    Executive or Central Committee at the earliest possible time.

THE WCC AND INTERNATIONAL BANKING IN
SOUTH AFRICA
(p. 37)

Following discussion, the Central Committee, on the recommendation of the
Reference Committee :

1. Instructed the Finance Department to communicate Document 31 (revised), with
    supporting documents, to the European-American Banking Corporation and its
    members, namely :

    The Deutsche Bank, Federal Republic of Germany
    The Société Générale, France
    The Midland Bank, United Kingdom

47

Amsterdam-Rotterdam Bank N.V., The Netherlands
The Société Générale de Banque S.A., Belgium
The Creditanstalt-Bankverein, Austria

and to solicit assurances that they will stop granting loans to the South African government and its agencies. It instructed the Finance Department to report the results to the Executive Committee and authorized the Executive Committee, if satisfactory assurances are not forthcoming, to ensure that no WCC funds are deposited with those banks.

2. Urged all member churches, Christian agencies and individual Christians, to use all their influence to press these above-mentioned banks and other banks participating in the loans to cease granting loans to the South African government and its agencies.

September 30, 1975

TO THE PARTICIPANTS IN THE FIFTH ASSEMBLY AT NAIROBI

Dear Friends,

As we are preparing ourselves for the Assembly, some have asked for advice about visiting South Africa before or after the Nairobi meetings.

In response to such inquiries, we would like to remind you that the South African government has since last year banned WCC Committee members and staff from visiting South Africa. This is characteristic of the government which has been selective in allowing Christian leaders to visit the country. In this connection, we share with you a moving letter from a South African in exile who raises pertinent questions about the ways in which those permitted to visit South Africa are unable to meet, or speak freely with the oppressed African people.

In the circumstances, it is evident that the government will continue to be selective in allowing Assembly participants to enter South Africa. Moreover, at a time when the Assembly is bound to express itself on the situation in Southern Africa, the possibility of making meaningful contact with Africans will be even more unlikely.

We, therefore, suggest that in the interest of solidarity, you should seriously consider whether it is appropriate to visit South Africa immediately before or after the Assembly even if you receive permission to do so. We are writing this and sending the enclosed letter simply to help you make your own decision.

Yours sincerely,

M. M. Thomas	Pauline M. Webb	Philip Potter
Chairman	Vice-Chairman	General Secretary

A WORD TO PROSPECTIVE CHURCH VISITORS TO SOUTH AFRICA

Dear Friends,

Over the years many overseas church visitors have come and gone to my country South Africa. They have come for a variety of reasons... to maintain links with sister denominations... to see for themselves what the situation is like in South Africa. This letter is an appeal to you not to go there, at least until we can freely invite you ourselves, under different circumstances in true fellowship. Why do I make such a request ?

In the first place you may not know how deceptive the system is in South Africa. In the silence of my brothers' and sisters' smiles you may not see their hearts torn with loneliness for their loved ones starving in the hated Bantustans (ironically called "homelands"). You will mistake the warm handshake for trust (we never know who is a police agent). We find it hard to speak openly and freely with you when you come to "visit" us when so many of our sisters and brothers have gone to jail because they spoke too freely and openly.

I have also noticed that the visitors from abroad have almost always been white and that you have taken the sincere observations of our white church representatives to be a true reflection of black feelings and aspirations. How could you know ? How can they know ? How many visitors will hear the voices of the banned, the banished, the hanged, the tortured, the imprisoned and the exiled ? How many church visitors have spoken to a few of the tens of thousands of prison labourers on the farms ? How many have sought to visit a jail or Robben Island ? How many have lived in a *kraal* and eaten our food with us instead of staying in "white only" hotels or rich suburban missionary homes ?

Did you know that our children die from starvation at the rate of one every minute, and that the average amount you spend on one such trip to South Africa is sufficient to feed fifteen children through a Kupugani feeding scheme for a period of 20 years ?

But the money you spend in our country will not go into such feeding schemes. It will only build bigger jails and buy more guns to suppress us. Meanwhile our children die daily — hourly.

Your presence in South Africa will be a continuous reminder to every black you see of the privileges they are denied daily. *You* will have freedom of movement and association. *You* will be able to use buses and elevators and restaurants forbidden to blacks. And short, you will be treated as a person.

What is it that you come to see in South Africa ? Forgive me for sounding so blunt but I don't understand. Do you come to see if the blacks are still suffering ? Is that something you must see with your own eyes before you'll believe it ? Are you looking for an exciting adventure ? (You may even take some risks whilst there — although you can always leave if it gets too hot). Isn't the information you seek already available from anti-apartheid groups in your own country ? If not, why can't you invite blacks to visit your church ?

We have often noticed how "factfinding" trips by church leaders have been used either by the South African government for propaganda, or by church spokespersons to discredit our liberation movements and our true leaders. This hurts.

If you care, please refuse to go. Do so as an act of solidarity with 80% of South Africa's people who have no freedom of travel in their own land. In solidarity with those who are banned, imprisoned, etc., and in solidarity with thousands of us who are in exile and cannot go home... yet.

If you will take this small step you will be supporting our struggle.

Thank you,
A South African in exile

STATEMENT FROM THE REPORT OF A CONSULTATION ORGANIZED BY THE COMMISSION ON FAITH AND ORDER AND THE PROGRAMME TO COMBAT RACISM — GENEVA — 14-20 SEPTEMBER, 1975

(pp. 6-8)

CHAPTER II : CHRISTIAN WITNESS AGAINST RACISM : COLLECTIVE REPENTANCE IN CORPORATE ACTION AND REFLECTION

1. The Gospel of Forgiveness and the Confession of Collective Sin

Some of us hold that it will only be possible to sustain the fight against racism if we start with the Gospel of grace and forgiveness. Our faith is in Jesus Christ who suffered on the Cross and through the Cross won the victory. He is the victorious victim. Out of the depth of his suffering he is the Lord of history, a history undercutting the histories of demonic oppression and of the evil revolt against God.

It is in this story that forgiveness and grace are always available and that new beginnings can be made. The witness of the foregoing grace in Jesus Christ must be the starting-point. Others are convinced that to begin with the Gospel of grace would leave us with the danger of belittling the sin of racism.

The first emphasis ought to be on confession. The Gospel of grace comes to those who truly repent. We must be aware of the fact that the word forgiveness can and has been used in an all too easy way : both asking and offering forgiveness can become an escape from the task of facing the depth of sin and the need for renewing action. There has been much cheap preaching of forgiveness which makes the term almost unbearable for many who have suffered from racist persecution.

We would affirm that it is essential to link both the Gospel of grace and the confession of sin very closely together. Because of the costly grace of Christ we are enabled to confess that racism is a sin which separates us from God and from our fellow human beings. Without it racism could be regarded as a disastrous fate which leaves us with despair or apathy.

We are obliged to confess that racism is a sin not only of individual Christians, but of churches and societies at large. To see the ubiquity of racism makes it mandatory to say that churches and peoples have become guilty of this sin.

The term "collective sin" is appropriate because it indicates that racism has so permeated the churches and the societies in which they are set that it has become part of the structure of ordinary life. People have become accustomed to patterns of neglect of and contempt for others, of injustice and prejudice, of degradation and exploitation and, now regard them as "normal". In the same way, churches have come to take for granted separations along lines of colour, to accept as "given" the divisions and barriers between people of different races. This demonic pervasiveness of racism compels us to speak of collective sin. "None is righteous, no not one" (Rom. 3:10). We are thrown together in a solidarity of sin. We are not free to dissociate ourselves self-righteously from this evil.

2. Corporate Repentance-Action

But even when we speak of collective sin with its evil ramifications, we are still within the sphere of Christ's sovereignty. Christ makes us free to repent. And we need indeed to repent. We are not brand racism as sin without at once responding to it with real and practical penitence.

This response involves repentance both at the individual level and at the corporate level, and repentance commits us to action. The two elements are intimately connected, which is why we prefer to speak of repentance-action or penitent action. But what is the appropriate action ?

Some, we know, define repentance in terms of compensatory action. We hesitate to adopt this solution, however, mainly because no material compensation could possibly repair all the immeasurable harm done in the past. To call for compensation in this sense would only be to belittle the suffering which has been caused. There is also the danger that such compensation would lead groups in the Third World to perpetuate their dependence on white churches. Moreover, compensatory action leads us to look backwards whereas repentance, we are convinced, moves forward, and is concerned not to restore the past but to seek a new and more just future. We have tried, therefore, to establish certain criteria for a forward looking active repentance which would do more justice to the still more radical imperative of the Gospel.

a) Ideally the *action* should not be unilateral but *decided by both parties,* oppressors and oppressed, *together.*

b) It should open up the possibility of *real community in the future.*

c) It should be *related to the wider area of racism in the secular and political field.*

d) Adherence to these criteria will *be costly.*

This means that repentance-action must be part of a deliberate effort to achieve a new kind of community, an effort which will call for radical changes not only in the administrative structures of the churches but also in society.

The political and economic implications will need to be spelt out and realistically faced, since privileged groups will inevitably have to forego some of their privileges.

In suggesting this idea of repentance-action, it is not supposed that such measures will eliminate all racist sins in the future. That is not within our power. What we envisage is action which can point effectively both to the reality of the sin we repent of and the new life we believe in. Repentance-action of this kind will not be unambiguous nor safe from misinterpretation. We could wish it were otherwise but the sad fact is that all our actions will inevitably bear the mark of the histories and structures in which we live and will therefore still sometimes have racist elements. There will always be a risk of making ourselves vulnerable on all sides.

3. The Church : Regrouping around Suffering

Discovering the sin of racism with all its implications and choosing the risky road of repentance-action, these are two aspects of one and the same process. It is a process which involves individuals and groups in the whole of their life and challenges their entire pattern of behaviour. But it is also a process which involves and challenges the Church of Christ in a preeminent way since there the message of forgiveness is spelt out and articulated as explicitly as possible. In this process we are driven to rethink our ideas as to the nature of the Church and to recover the meaning and implications of its original mission.

We have tried to set out some criteria for "repentance-action". Basically, these criteria reflect an attempt to find a new understanding and new forms of discipleship, but not simply in view of the need to combat racism. It is a more radical challenge than that which confronts the churches. We have to go back to the roots and try to restate the real meaning of discipleship. The criteria we found all point to one thing, namely, the need to re-establish community in situations where there is suffering. This should be our starting point for redefining discipleship.

STATEMENTS FROM THE FIFTH ASSEMBLY OF THE WORLD COUNCIL OF CHURCHES NAIROBI (1975)

REPORT OF SECTION V : STRUCTURES OF INJUSTICE AND STRUGGLES FOR LIBERAION

Racism

Fundamental Convictions (pp. 109-113)

57. Racism is a sin against God and against fellow human beings. It is contrary to the justice and the love of God revealed in Jesus Christ. It destroys the human dignity of both the racist and the victim. When practised by Christians it denies the very faith we profess and undoes the credibility of the Church and its witness to Jesus Christ. Therefore, we condemn racism in all its forms both inside and outside the Church.

58. When we again try to deal with racism at this Assembly we cannot but begin by confessing our conscious and unconscious complicity in racism and our failures to eradicate it even from our own house. In previous Assemblies we have many times affirmed as churches our common rejection of racism. Yet, we still find ourselves only at the beginning. We stand in need of God's forgiveness and grace which will free us from our complicity and failures, towards a new commitment, to strive for the justice that will bring an end to all racism.

59. The past years of struggle against racism have shown that we as churches need a more profound understanding of the nature and of all varied manifestations of racism. We need to confront it with the fullness of the biblical message, to see more deeply its demonic character, and also to comprehend its psychological, economic and social impact on persons and communities and its roots in societies. However, although our understanding needs to grow, we already know more than enough to participate in obedience to Christ in the fight against the manifestations of racism in politics and in the Church.

60. Concerning the methods to be used in the fight against racism, we join the agonizing search for guidelines on how to deal with the inevitable question of violence and non-violence. A helpful contribution to this search has been made in the paper "Violence, Non-violence, and the Struggle for Social Justice" (commended by the WCC Central Committee, 1973).

The scope of Racism — A Litany of Shame

61. Racism can be seen today in every part of the world. No nation is totally free of it. Its victims cross the paths of most of us daily. Yet, it is obvious that some of our countries are more visibly plagued by it than others, e.g. : where racism is legally enforced. We heard in the Section from every continent a series of passionate pleas to draw the common attention of the churches here to the outrageous expression of racism in their respective countries, like a litany of shame of the whole human family. However, it brought home the growing urgency of the problem of racism on every continent.

62. There is much evidence that racially oppressed communities are rapidly becoming aware of the injustices to which they are subjected and that they more and more refuse to endure indignity and exploitation. Consequently, they are increasingly determined to liberate themselves and thereby affirm their humanity. We need to express our solidarity with them.

63. It also became obvious that racism is a factor in numerous violations of human rights and fundamental freedoms as dealt with in another part of this Report.

Racism in Churches

64. To our shame, Christian churches around the world are all too often infected by racism, overt and covert. Examples of it include the following :

(a) churches and congregations have been and are still being organized along racially exclusive lines;

(b) congregations welcome to their fellowship warmly those who are like the majority of its members, but easily reject those who are different;

(c) many argue that they are free of racism as if its reality could be undone by ignoring it;

(d) churches frequently contribute to the psychological conditioning of the racially oppressed so that they will not sense the racism imposed upon them;

(e) they are more willing to support struggles against racism far from home than to face the racism which is practised on their doorstep;

(f) churches often reflect the racially prejudiced attitudes of their governments, their elites, and self-pretensions, while presuming that their own attitudes arise out of Christian faith;

(g) in leadership privileges and in programmatic priorities churches tend too easily to indulge in racism without even recognizing it.

65. We recognize that the Spirit of God does break through structural and other barriers so that Christian communities do from time to time rise to challenge their own racism and to seek models of commitment to a non-racist Christian faith, even if for every such sign of hope there remain too many examples of denial.

Institutional Racism

66. Pervasive as individual attitudes and acts of racism may be, the major oppressive racism of our time is imbedded in institutional structures that reinforce and perpetuate themselves, generally to the great advantage of the few and the disadvantage of many. Examples of this :

(a) racism openly enforced by law;

(b) predominantly white North Atlantic nations create trade patterns and preferences that militate against other racial groups;

(c) strong military powers and other industrialized countries supply sophisticated arms and assistance to racist regimes;

(d) powerful countries, without regard to their social system, often entrench themselves in supporting racial repression under the pretence of legally justified defence of their own national self-interest;

(e) continued patterns of settler colonialism contribute to racial oppression;

(f) the powerful in affluence, education, ecclesiastical position, or secular authority, tend to protect their systems of privilege and to shut out of the decision-making any influence of the weak and the subordinate. Moreover, they tend to overlay their racist privileges all too often with an aura of kindliness and service.

67. Institutionalized racism, in its many structural forms, resists most challenges with careful concessions calculated to preserve its power. We reject a conspiratorial theory of history that oversimplifies the complex struggles of humanity for liberation by describing all institutions with power as pernicious and all powerless peoples as virtuous. This does not, however, make us blind to the evident inclination of current power structures to perpetuate racism. All these institutional forms of racism need to be carefully analysed and as Christians we need to attack them with prophetic word and action.

Interdependence of Oppression

68. We lift up for special attention the fact that across the globe racist structures reinforce each other internationally. Self-serving policies of transnational corporations operate across boundaries with impunity; weapons or mercenaries are supplied internationally to local elites; the worldwide communications networks are manipulated to reinforce racist attitudes and actions. It is precisely because of this worldwide web or racist penetration that the churches must seek out policies and programmes at ecumenical and international levels. Such programmes can expose international systems which support racism and provide an effective counter-response to them.

69. In this connection it should be noted that churches and their foreign mission agencies in the West ought to re-examine their use of human and material resources so that they can effectively support liberation efforts and contribute to human dignity in developing countries in ways that are beyond the scope of traditional patterns of giving and receiving.

70. The multinational character of racist structures also makes necessary a constant vigilance by Christians so that they are ready to speak and act and that pressure of international challenges to racism is felt and felt strongly, and the victims of racism may know that they are not abandoned and that their liberation is essential to the liberation of all.

The Urgency of the Task of the Churches

71. The grip of racism is today as acute as ever because of its institutional penetration, its reinforcement by military and economic power and because of widespread fear of loss of privilege by the affluent world.

72. This gives a special urgency to the task of the churches both in facing and eradicating racism within themselves and their home countries and in strengthening their international efforts against racism.

73. Southern Africa deserves continued priority in the churches' combined efforts because of the churches' own involvement in the area and because of the legal enforcement of racism there. African delegates brought forcefully before us the need of churches to practise what they preach. What is at stake is the faithfulness to the fullness of the message entrusted to the Church.

Recommendations on Racism adopted by the Assembly (pp. 118-119)

83. We commend the Programme to Combat Racism to the member churches, and urge them to ensure that their members receive accurate information about the whole programme. We ask for further support of the Programme in terms of increased commitment, prayer, and finance, in order that the various aspects of the Programme, e.g. : theological reflection, action-oriented research, information, Annual Project List and Special Fund, may be even more effective.

84. Of primary importance to the churches' involvement in the struggle against racism is theological reflection on racism and on methods of combating it. We therefore draw to the churches' attention the ongoing joint project of the Programme to Combat Racism and Faith and Order and its report on a recent consultation, "Racism in Theology and Theology against Racism" (WCC 1975). We also encourage the study and implementation of the report on "Violence, Non-violence, and the Struggle for Social Justice", commended to the member churches by the Central Committee (Geneva 1973).

85. We urge member churches to ensure, wherever possible, the active participation of representatives from minority and racially oppressed groups in decision-making concerning their welfare and well-being within the life of churches and of society.

86. We urge member churches to provide factual information, gained from the oppressed groups themselves, so that Christians can learn the extent of their involvement in structures that perpetuate racial injustice and have recourse to specific proposals for responsible ecumenical action.

87. South Africa, which highlights racism in its most blatant forms, must retain high priority for the attention of the member churches. Apartheid is possible only with the support of a large number of Christians there. We urge member churches to identify with, and wherever possible initiate or activate, campaigns to halt arms traffic; to work for the withdrawal of investments and the ending of bank loans; to stop white migration. These issues have already been urged by the WCC and we recommend these for urgent action by the member churches. Their implementation would be an effective non-violent contribution to the struggle against racism.

88. Racism, as a world problem, however, also demands the churches' attention in other particular situations, including

(a) the plight of the Korean minority in Japan;

(b) the condition of the native peoples of North and South America;

(c) the situation of the Aboriginal peoples of Australia and ethnic minorities in New Zealand;

(d) growing racism against black people and migrant workers in Europe.

89. Churches everywhere should beware that their commendable zeal for combatting racism and other forms of ethnocentrism in distant lands should not lead to ignoring its manifestations in their midst.

90. In all this, churches should be making a conscious effort to be themselves models of non-racist communities.

NUCLEAR COLLABORATION WITH SOUTH AFRICA

(pp. 167-169)

1. The Fifth Assembly expresses its deep concern that certain governments and multi-national companies are becoming involved in the financing and construction of nuclear power generating plants in South Africa. Those countries and companies known to us to be taking part are :

(a) General Electric, *USA*;

(b) Rijn-Schelde-Verolme Machinefabrieken en Scheepswerwen N.V. (R.S.V.); Verenigde Bedrijven Bredero N.V. (V.B.B.); Ingenieursbureau Comprimo N.V., *Netherlands*;

(c) Brown-Boveri International Corporation, *Switzerland*;

(d) Kraftwerk Union (K.W.U.), *Federal Republic of Germany* (Participants : Siemens and A.E.G.);

(e) Framatome, *France* (Participants : Creusot-Loire group and Westinghouse-USA).

2. The technical expertise and commercial benefits rest with the companies, but the normal official and financial requirements covering export licences and credit guarantees are the responsibility of the national governments concerned. Acceptance of one or two of the tenders now under preparation with endorsement by the relevant governments will result in a further economic and financial undergirding of apartheid. Furthermore, Western technological expertise is assisting South Africa in the development of a nuclear enrichment plant which will make South Africa self-sufficient in

nuclear fuel for civil and military use. Economic and industrial resources in the West will thus be still more intimately committed to the expansion of a system which denies to the majority of the inhabitants the prospect or right of personal, social, and political freedom.

3. The Assembly is further concerned at the military implications of these nuclear developments, especially since South Africa is not a signatory power to the Non-Proliferation Treaty. South Africa's military expenditures has increased from R 255 million (US dollars 300 million) in 1965/1966 to over R 1000 million (US dollars 1200 million) in 1975/1976; nuclear power plants and nuclear enrichment plants will facilitate development of nuclear weapons. Already there are grave fears of South African military activity beyond its borders, previously in Zimbabwe and now in Angola as well as Namibia. Any implied condoning of this military capability by any governments or company will precipitate serious anxiety and strong objections on the part of the people throughout Africa.

4. The WCC calls on its member churches in those countries involved to :

(a) ascertain the extent of their own country's commercial and governmental commitment to South Africa's nuclear programme;

(b) make public the political and military implication and consequences of pursuing a policy of collaboration with the South African authorities;

(c) challenge those companies and governments involved to revise their policies in the light of considerations which are broader than the commercial and economic criteria involved.

STATEMENT FROM THE CENTRAL COMMITTEE, GENEVA (1976)

The Transkei (and Bantustans - "Homelands") (pp. 46-48)

The Central Committee adopted the following statement :

On 26 October 1976 the South African government intends to declare the Transkei "independent", the first of South Africa's Bantustans to be so designated. This would be the "national home" of all Xhosa-speaking Africans in the country, with the exception of those deemed to belong to the Ciskei Bantustan. The Transkei's present population of about 1.7 million people would in theory swell to around 3 million when all those obliged to assume its citizenship are included.

The concept which underlies the creation of the "independent" Transkei (and of the other nine Bantustans, each destined for eventual "independence") is based on the notion of supposed "tribal" or "national" identities which are racially determined. It creates artifical divisions within the African population and between them and other South Africans. It is rooted in the doctrine of apartheid. In theory and in practice the Bantustans encapsulate apartheid, and their recognition as "independent" entities would clear the way for the emergence of a South Africa with no black citizens at all.

The South African government is insisting that on "independence" all Transkeian citizens, many of whom were born in urban South Africa and have never seen the Transkei, shall surrender their South African citizenship and become citizens of the Transkei alone. They will thus be obliged to surrender against their will for all time any share in by far the greater part of the wealth which has been created through their labour and the space of their own country. Therefore, the political function of the "independent" Transkei would be to serve as the first of the enclaves within which the African people would be allowed in principle to exercise their civil rights on condition that they abandon their birthright.

The underdevelopment and overpopulation of the Transkei mean that it will be forced to continue to depend upon the evil system of migratory labour in order to avoid even more desperate poverty. This dependence dovetails neatly with the dependence of the white South African economy on an abundant supply of cheap labour, and so the economic function of the "independent" Transkei would be to serve as a labour reservoir.

The Xhosa-speaking people had expected to enjoy full political rights within South Africa. They oppose the exchange of their South African citizenship for citizenship of the Transkei. They had no say in the unilateral decision of the white Parliament to create the Bantustans and to deprive them of their rights as citizens of South Africa.

The Central Committee of the World Council of Churches, recalling that the WCC has on many occasions declared its opposition to apartheid and to racism as being contrary to the Gospel and incompatible with the nature of the Church of Christ and violating basic human rights, therefore :

condemns the deceptive manoeuvre of the South African government to perpetuate and consolidate apartheid by the creation of the so-called "independent" Transkei, by which these three million South Africans will be made foreigners in their own country;

condemns any other policy which would further isolate and divide the African population;

calls on member churches of the WCC to expose the evil of the Bantustan policy;

recommends in this connection to member churches for their study and for further dissemination of information the booklet *South Africa's Bantustans : What Independence for the Transkei ?*, published by the Programme to Combat Racism of the WCC;

calls on member churches to urge their governments to oppose the Bantustan policy, to withhold recognition of the Transkei as an independent state and to have no direct or indirect diplomatic, commercial or other relations with the Transkei, or any other activity which would imply recognition; and

expresses its solidarity with and compassion for the Xhosa-speaking people as they struggle for the legitimate rights of all Africans in South Africa.

Southern Africa (pp. 44-46)

The Central Committee then adopted the following statement :

The liberation struggle in Southern Africa has entered a new and crucial state. The intensification of the war in Zimbabwe (Rhodesia), the deadline given by the Security Council of the United Nations to comply with its directives on Namibia and the uprisings in South Africa all denote significant new phases in the struggle for freedom and dignity in these countries. The Central Committee recalls the statement of the Fifth Assembly (report of Section V) that "Southern Africa deserves continued priority in the churches' combined efforts because of the churches' own involvement in the area and because of the legal enforcement of racism there. What is at stake is the faithfulness to the fullness of the message entrusted to the Church".

I. Zimbabwe

In Zimbabwe the collapse of the "constitutional talks", the closure of the Mozambique border and the intensification of the armed struggle by the freedom fighters are highly significant developments. As a recent report of the International Commission of Jurists has shown conclusively, the policies of the illegal Rhodesian regime are "the intensification of the repression and growing adoption by Southern Rhodesia of the laws and values of the apartheid system in South Africa".

The Central Committee of the World Council of Churches :

expresses grave concern at the continued oppression of the people of Zimbabwe by the illegal regime, the arbitrary imprisonment and detention of political leaders and others, the execution of freedom fighters, the criminal measures of collective punishment and the continued denial of human rights, under the disguise of the so-called preservation of Western civilization;

calls upon the member churches to intensify their efforts to mobilize public opinion in favour of the liberation of Zimbabwe and to extend to the people of Zimbabwe all the moral, political and humanitarian assistance necessary in their struggle for the achievement of their right to self-determination and independence.

II. Namibia

South Africa, which illegally occupies Namibia, has been asked by the Security Council of the United Nations by its Resolution No. 385 to comply by 31 August 1976 with its directives to respect Namibia's territorial integrity and to declare its intention to hold free national elections on the basis of universal suffrage under UN supervision. Far from respecting this directive, the South African government under the facade of the so-called constitutional conference has unleashed a reign of terror in the country which it illegally occupies and is pursuing a policy of "bantustanization" which attempts to divide the Namibians when they seek unity.

The Central Committee of the World Council of Churches :

calls upon the South African government to comply with the UN directives with regard to Namibia and the UN recognition of SWAPO as the authentic representative of the people of Namibia; to release all Namibian political prisoners, including all those imprisoned or detained in connection with offences under so-called internal security laws; and

calls upon the member churches :

a) to increase their support to the people of Namibia in their struggle for liberation, to spread information about the situation, to make intercession for the people and to give appropriate and meaningful aid;

b) to ask their governments to support effectively the UN directives regarding Namibia;

c) to intensify action against Western military and economic collaboration with South Africa with its grave implications for Namibia; and

d) to encourage their members to participate in the International Week of Solidarity with the people of Namibia beginning on 27 October 1976.

III.   South Africa

The liberation struggle in South Africa has entered a new phase with the recent revolt which erupted in Soweto and has spread to many parts of the country. The white regime has tried to suppress this revolt with ruthless and horrific measures and there has been a very heavy toll of human life. These uprisings are a manifestation of the new momentum of the struggle for freedom and dignity in South Africa.

South Africa's enormous militarism and its reinforcement by active military and economic cooperation with major Western powers constitute a major threat to peace. This threat is intensified by the recent Franco-South African agreement on nuclear collaboration.

The Central Committee of the World Council of Churches reiterates the statement of the Acting General Secretary about the Soweto massacre of 18 June 1976, and in deep concern for all people in South Africa who are suffering in this situation :

calls upon the South African regime to end violence against the oppressed majority, to recognize immediately their full human rights, to release forthwith all those imprisoned for political reasons, and to abandon apartheid; and

urges all member churches and particularly the churches in South Africa to do everything in their power to counteract the repressive violence of the regime and to demonstrate by action their solidarity with the oppressed; and

urges member churches in countries which maintain military and economic links with South Africa to press their governments to end this collaboration; and to intensify their efforts to discourage white emigration to South Africa, by urging the press and other agencies not to accept advertisements for or to recruit white labour for South Africa.

PRIORITIES FOR PCR AS RECOMMENDED BY THE REVIEW COMMITTEE AND ADOPTED BY THE CENTRAL COMMITTEE

Programme to Combat racism (PCR) (p. 102)

1. Southern Africa should continue as the major focus for the present period.

2. Work with Latin American Indians should be given major emphasis at this point, with its duration being reviewed in 1979.

3. Land rights of racial minorities should be an immediate focus, also for review in 1979.

4. The important but complex issue of racism in Asia should be explored at this point with a view to its being given major emphasis in 1979.

5. PCR should play a supportive role to those who are already acting on the race issue in North America and Europe.

6. The Special Fund should be continued.

CRITERIA FOR THE SPECIAL FUND TO COMBAT RACISM AS REAFFIRMED
(after a slight change of wording) (p. 111)

1. The purpose of the organizations must not be in conflict with the general purposes of the WCC and its units, and the grants are to be used for humanitarian activities (i.e : social, health and educational purpose, legal aid, etc.).

2. The proceeds of the Fund shall be used to support organizations that combat racism, rather than welfare organizations that alleviate the effects of racism and which would normally be eligible for support from other units of the World Council of Churches.

3. a) The focus of the grants should be on raising the level of awareness and on strengthening the organizational capability of the racially oppressed people

   b) In addition we recognize the need to support organizations that align themselves with the victims of racial injustice and pursue the same objectives.

4. The grants are made without control of the manner in which they are spent, and are intended as an expression of commitment by the PCR to the cause of economic, social and political justice, which these organizations promote.

5. a) The situation in Southern Africa is recognized as a priority due to the overt and intensive nature of white racism and the increasing awareness on the part of the oppressed in their struggle for liberation.

b) In the selection of other areas we have taken account of those places where the struggle is most intense and where a grant might make a substantial contribution to the process of liberation, particularly where racial groups are in imminent danger of being physically or culturally exterminated.

c) In considering applications from organizations in countries of white and affluent majorites, we have taken note only of those where political involvement precludes help from other sources.

6. Grants should be made with due regard to where they can have the maximum effect : token grants should not be made unless there is a possibility of their eliciting a substantial response from other organizations.

STATEMENT FROM THE EXECUTIVE COMMITTEE, GENEVA (1977)

Bank Loans to South Africa (p. 7)

The Executive Committee

recalls the decision of the WCC Central Committee taken in August 1972 to deposit none of its funds in banks which maintain direct banking operations in South Africa;

recalls the decision of the WCC Executive Committee, taken in November 1975, to deposit none of its funds with the European American Banking Corporation and its six member banks in the light of their refusal to give assurances that they would stop granting loans to the South African government and its agencies;

learns from the Dutch PCR support group "Prepaid Reply" that the Dutch bank with which the WCC has an account — the Algemene Bank Nederland — has admitted in the autumn of 1976 that it has been making loans to the South African government and its agencies under conditions similar to those which obtained in the case of the EABC loans, despite its earlier denials that it had made any such loans;

commends the initiatives taken by "Prepaid Reply" to uncover and discourage Dutch banking operations which directly support apartheid;

expresses deep disappointment about the ABN having made loans to the South African government and its agencies and about the fact that the ABN has given incorrect information about these loans;

decides that an assurance be sollicited from the ABN that it will stop granting loans to the South African government and its agencies until legally enforced racism in South Africa has been abolished;

authorized the WCC Officers, if a satisfactory assurance is not forthcoming by 1 May 1977, to withdraw WCC funds deposited with the ABN after that date.

(This assurance was received from the ABN as well as AMRO, another major Dutch bank.)

STATEMENT FROM THE CENTRAL COMMITTEE, GENEVA (1977)

Southern Africa (pp. 35-38)

The Central Committee adopted the following resolutions :

We, the Central Committee of the World Council of Churches, as a concerned body of Christians, and in faithfulness to the Gospel denounce as blasphemous the grave and blatant injustices being perpetrated in the name of "Christian civilization" by the governments and powerful oppressors of Southern Africa, in Zimbabwe, Namibia and the Republic of South Africa.

The future of the oppressed people of Southern Africa should be a matter for their decision and for theirs alone. The past year has seen an intensification of the liberation struggle in Southern Africa which has led to increased repression. That, in human terms, means an increase in violence, disruption of family life, and widespread suffering. The situation is tragic and volatile because interests outside Africa insist by their actions that it is they who will decide the future rather than the oppressed people of Southern Africa. We recommend to the member churches the following actions :

— to reiterate and demonstrate their solidarity with the oppressed people of the region in their just struggle for self-determination and independence, and constantly to make intercession for them;

— to support groups which are mobilizing public opinion about the reality of Southern Africa, and working for change there and to join them in pressing for the ending of all support — military, economic, diplomatic and cultural — for the white minority governments;

— to express grave concern at the explosive implications of the reported scheme of the Bolivian government to receive white settlers en masse from Southern Africa to Latin America, recognizing that this would constitute a threat to the indigenous people of the Latin American continent;

— to call attention to the fact that any mass migration of white settlers from Southern Africa would simply encourage the transfer of racism to another society;

64

— to call in Christian witness on the white people within Southern Africa to change their mind, to renounce their position of racial privilege and to dedicate themselves alongside all the peoples of Southern Africa to the building of a just society there.

Zimbabwe

Since the last meeting of the Central Committee, the abortive Geneva conference has given way to a series of Western initiatives towards a negotiated settlement, none of which has so far come near to success in making the illegal minority regime cede control to the Zimbabwean people. The regime will relinquish power only when it is forced to the point that it has no other alternative. Its pursuit of a so-called internal settlement and its announcement of a date for an election are manoeuvres to disguise its determination to retain the initiative.

The Central Committee of the World Council of Churches :

— *denounces again* the continued oppression of the people of Zimbabwe by the illegal regime, arbitrary imprisonment and detention, the execution of Zimbabweans, the criminal measures of collective punishment and the continued denial of human rights under the guise of the preservation of so-called Western "Christian" civilization;

— *repeats* its call to member churches to intensify their efforts to mobilize public opinion in favour of the liberation of Zimbabwe, and to extend to the people of Zimbabwe all the moral, political and humanitarian assistance necessary in their struggle for the realization of their right to self-determination and independence;

— *condemns* the illegal regime's aggression against neighbouring countries, which is additionally a strategy designed to make the hostilities international and to involve the great powers;

— *calls upon* member churches to bring pressure to bear either by divesting themselves of their shares or by shareholder action upon Mobil, Shell, BP, Total, Caltex and all other oil companies involved, to put an end to the illegal sales of their products, direct or indirect, by the companies themselves or through their subsidiairies or other intermediaries, to the Rhodesian regime; and

— *calls upon* member churches to urge their governments to treat enlistment in the armed forces, of the illegal Rhodesian regime, as a criminal offence, to punish offenders accordingly, and to outlaw any recruitment for this purpose.

Namibia

Four Namibian church leaders wrote to Dr Henry Kissinger on 18 June, 1976. Their letter included this sentence : "... We are convinced that the vast majority of the black population of our country fervently desires that the South African police, army and administration should rapidly leave this country..." There is, if anything, even more evidence of the truth of that statement today than there was a year ago. The Western powers' attempts to agree a solution with Mr Vorster are not in the context of UN

Security Council Resolution 385 and therefore must be seen as designed to retain the initiative for determining both the pace and the nature of change in Namibia in hands which are not Namibian (Resolution 385 calls inter alia for the holding in Namibia of free elections, under UN supervision and control, throughout the country as one political entity, and demands the unconditional release of all Namibian political prisoners and the withdrawal of the South African administration).

The Central Committee of the World Council of Churches :

— *reaffirms* its solidarity in Christian witness with the churches and people of Namibia and calls on member churches to support them in every way, by making intercession, spreading information and giving necessary aid;

— *calls upon* member churches to press their governments and the South African Government to comply with UN Security Council Resolution 385 and the UN recognition of SWAPO as the authentic representative of the Namibian people, and

— *calls upon* the South African Government to stop the torture of Namibians, to release unconditionally all Namibian political prisoners, wherever they are held, to end its policy of forced resettlement of the country's people, and to withdraw its army and police from Namibia well before the election date.

South Africa

The worsening repression perpetrated by the government of South Africa shows that it is not concerned to talk or to listen to black people except on its own terms, and that more often it bans, detains, imprisons, tortures and kills them. But, there is a growing dialogue between the South African Government and the major powers — a dialogue in words and a traffic in money and arms.

The Central Committee of the World Council of Churches, in our Christian witness :

— *honours* those Christians of all races in South Africa who have — sometimes against great odds — sought to be faithful to the demands of the Gospel by their prophetic witness in the South African situation, and encourages them to continue to do everything in their power to counter the repressive violence of the regime and to demonstrate by action their solidarity with the oppressed; and

— *calls upon* the member churches within and outside South Africa to press the South African regime urgently to end violence against the oppressed majority, to recognize immediately their full human rights, to release at once all political prisoners, and to abandon apartheid, including the existence of bantustans;

— *urges* member churches to work for the imposition of a mandatory and complete arms embargo against South Africa and the withdrawal of licences for the manufacture of arms, noting in particular the significance of arms exports from the USA, Britain, the FRG, France, Italy and Israel, and the continued existence of cultural accords between South Africa and Belgium, the Netherlands and the FRG; and

66

— *rejects* as irrelevant changes such as those proposed in the Statement of Principles issued in March 1977 by US companies operating in South Africa, because they only achieve special treatment of a few while ignoring the continued exploitation of the majority;

— *calls* on member churches to urge their governments and regional groupings, especially the European Economic Community, North America and the Commonwealth, to take specific steps which will ensure the stopping of export credit guarantees and bank loans to and investments in the Republic of South Africa.

STATEMENT FROM THE CENTRAL COMMITTEE, KINGSTON, JAMAICA (1979)

(pp. 58-61)

Recommendations

It is accordingly recommended that :

2. The Central Committee resolves, in the light of changing circumstances and escalation of racism, to accept the proposal of the General Secretary that a process of consultation — to be set in motion as soon as possible — on how the churches may be involved in combating racism in the 1980's, be given priority. In doing this, account should be taken of the experience gained, the questions raised and the criticisms made during the ten years of existence of this programme.

The process of consultation should include meetings having a balanced representation and involving :

a) representatives of the member churches;

b) representatives of race relations' desks of member churches, national and regional councils;

c) representatives of the racially oppressed.

This process should include a major consultation whose recommendations and deliberations should be made available to the Central Committee in 1980.

Since many of the questions and criticisms raised are to be found in the Central Committee background paper on Southern Africa, particularly Part III on "Issues and Dilemmas in the Present Debate", and the Unit II Committee document containing an evaluation of the background paper "South Africa's Hope — What Price Now ?", these papers among others should form a basis for consultation and discussion as suggested above, without restricting them to the Southern Africa situation.

3. The financial implications of this process of consultation should be considered by the Finance Committee at the Central Committee.

4. The General Secretary should be requested to report to the Executive Committee in September 1979 on the progress made.

Investments, trade and bank loans to South Africa

The Central Committee reaffirms its request to PCR to give special attention to the issues of investments and trade (Central Committee, Utrecht 1972), bank loans to South Africa (Central Committee, West Berlin 1974) at this time when foreign economic interests stand out as a major factor favouring the maintenance and strengthening of apartheid, and also when several member churches and church groups are becoming increasingly involved in campaigns against investments in South Africa and boycott the consumer goods from that country. The Central Committee therefore urges renewed PCR concentration on these issues.

Organized white mass migration from Southern Africa

Oppressed racial groups and churches continue to express concern about the organized white mass migration from Southern Africa to a number of countries in North and Latin America, Western Europe, Australia and New Zealand.

In 1977 the Central Committee recommended to the member churches the following actions :

— "to express grave concern at the explosive implications of the reported scheme of the Bolivian government to receive white settlers en masse from Southern Africa to Latin America, recognizing that this would constitute a threat to the indigenous people of the Latin American continent;

— to call attention to the fact that any mass migration of white settlers from Southern Africa would simply encourage the transfer of racism to another society."

It is therefore recommended that :

PCR in cooperation with other sub-units, including the Migration Secretariat, should intensify its investigation into, and action on, the issue of organized white mass migration from Southern Africa, especially into those countries with racially oppressed peoples.

Racism in children's and school textbooks

The Unit Committee strongly commends PCR's efforts to combat racism in children's and school textbooks as well as in Christian educational material. The report and study guide of a first regional workshop should be sent to all member churches and national and regional councils for their consideration and action.

Racism in Asia

The Central Committee in 1976 requested PCR to give major attention to racism in Asia as of 1979. In 1977, the Central Committee recommended that "regional ecumenical bodies be involved in the development of PCR's agenda". In pursuance of this recommendation a workshop was held in Auckland, New Zealand, in 1978 on "Race and Minority Issues in Asia", sponsored by WCC/PCR and CCA/Urban Rural Mission.

The workshop gathered 45 people from 12 countries and dealt with a wide variety of issues, including minority rights, race identity, national unity, justice and participation. The workshop made recommendations and urged the churches to stand in solidarity with racially oppressed minorities in Asia.

The Central Committee requests PCR to continue to work with CCA/URM and member churches in the area on race and minority issues, including :

a) collection and publication of testimonies on land and life experience in the struggle for justice;

b) production and distribution of audiovisual aid material for educational purposes;

c) sponsoring of further workshops and training possibilities to improve the organizational capability of racially oppressed minorities.

Land rights and racially oppressed indigenous people

a) The Central Committee receives the document on "Land Rights and Racially Oppressed Indigenous Peoples" with particular emphasis on the situations in Australia and Brazil, as the first result of PCR's research for action programme in this area. It requests that information on the issue be made available to the member churches and that further cooperation be worked out with the churches in Australia and Brazil.

b) The Central Committee requests PCR to indicate a plan of action together with all the churches in Australia and Brazil, and particularly with organizations of the racially oppressed and support groups in these countries. This plan of action should promote further research and plans of action in these countries.

c) The Central Committee requests that serious attention be given to adequate staffing for this next stage of the programme.

The Unit Committee reminded the Central Committee that since May 1978 the PCR Commission had been requesting supporters of the Special Fund to make an additional 10% grant in order to cover the costs of administration of the Fund. It noted that the response to this request had been positive and that present income designated for this purpose covered the administrative costs. The Central Committee endorsed this line of action and requested the Finance Department to indicate separately the figures concerned.

STATEMENT FROM THE CENTRAL COMMITTEE, GENEVA (1980)

(pp. 57-61)

The Central Committee :

a) expressed deep gratitude for the prompt and widespread response by the member churches to the call for consultation at national and regional level;

b) commended to the member churches for wide distribution and careful study both the reports of the national and regional consultations and the report of the WCC world consultation;

c) called attention to the background papers prepared for those consultations which contain important supplementary resource material for the thorough study of racism.

The Central Committee noted that from this consultation process the following issues had emerged as requiring greater emphasis and response as part of the total commitment to combat racism in the 1980s :

a) the all-pervasive and diverse nature of racism : there is no society that is intrinsically immune to the cancer of racism; it manifests itself in many different forms, including tribalism, caste and discrimination against people of any different ethnic origin;

b) the infection of the churches themselves with racism : the churches in their structures and practices too often reflect the sins of the societies in which they are set;

c) the interlocking of racism and political and economic domination : combating racism means confronting the realities of the international economic order, the struggle of the superpowers for supremacy and the repressive apparatus employed in the interest of so-called "national security".

Yet in the midst of a worldwide escalation of racism there were grounds for hope in :

a) the progress being made by the oppressed towards their liberation : in all consultations oppressed people reported on the struggles in which they are engaged, demonstrating a higher level of awareness, a greater organizational capability and a stronger sense of international solidarity;

b) the increasing participation of churches and Christians in the combating of racism : the conviction that racism is a perversion of God's creation and an obstacle to the churches' mission is being more clearly and strongly expressed and initiatives against racism are receiving increasing support from the Christian community.

In the past 11 years the churches' role in combating racism had been in the world's eyes focused primarily in the WCC's own Programme to Combat Racism. As we entered a new phase, it must be made evident that this combat had a high priority on the agenda of all churches in their witness to the Gospel of Christ.

Therefore the Central Committee :

a) called on member churches to declare as a fundamental matter of faith that the doctrine and practice of apartheid is a perversion of the Christian Gospel (through a confession of faith, covenant, "status confessionis" or equivalent commitment);

b) urged member churches, in obedience to their faith, to examine in penitence their own involvement in racism, wherever and whatever form it occurs;

c) invited member churches to match their actions to the following imperatives which have come from the consultations :

— listen to the racially oppressed; they define the direction of the struggle;

— support organizations of the racially oppressed, respecting their self-reliance; make available money, land, resources and publicity;

— encourage research programmes; give priority to research conducted by the racially oppressed;

— reject apartheid; support sanctions against South Africa and work for the withdrawal of investments and bank loans;

— scrutinize legislation; national security laws, migration laws and their enforcement are often either overtly or covertly racially oppressive;

— publicize the struggle against racism; encourage the investigation and exposure of racial exploitation and the counter-acting of racism in the media;

— challenge theology; does it merely conform to or does it transcend and help to transform the society it comes out of ?

— change church structures; they should be more inclusive of all groups in the community they serve and more responsive to them;

— mobilize people in the churches; help them to be effectively active rather than guilty passive in their opposition to racism;

— internationalize the issues; encourage learning about and linking up with others combating racism in other regions and at the global level.

Action by the World Council of Churches

In determining its own action in response to the recommendations coming from the consultation process, the Central Committee noted that :

a) all consultations without exception had recommended that the present mandate of the Programme to Combat Racism be reaffirmed;

b) the criteria and functioning of the Special Fund had been extensively discussed and after consideration of the criticisms it had evoked, the Special Fund in its present form had been commended by an overwhelming majority;

c) some consultations including the world consultation, had recommended that PCR's areas of attention be widened to emphasize other forms of racism as well as white racism;

d) the process had facilitated closer cooperation between member churches themselves, as well as between member churches and the PCR; churches, national and regional councils had indicated their determination to accept increased responsibilities in the field of racial justice;

e) while the national and regional consultations allowed particular insights to be gained, the holding of a final world consultation had enabled these to be drawn together and some world perspectives developed;

f) the personal encounter with oppressed peoples had radically changed the perception of many participants in the consultation, who would never again see opposing racism in merely academic terms.

In the light of these considerations the Central Committee resolved :

a) to reaffirm the Programme to Combat Racism;

b) to continue the Special Fund under its present criteria, and through the Executive Committee to work with the PCR Commission in maintaining the Fund's effectiveness as an instrument of the whole programme;

c) to commend to the member churches increased support for the PCR's operating budget, its Programme Project List and the Special Fund.

There was one abstention in the vote on the first resolution, 7 on the second and 6 on the third.

In order to implement the recommendations coming from the consultation process the Central Committee requested the PCR :

1. **To assist national and regional church initiatives**

By providing or facilitating :

— analyses and information about specific situations;

— ecumenical team visits to areas requiring particular attention;

— contacts with racially oppressed groups;

— international contacts to help widen perspectives;

— financial support.

2. To be directly involved from a world perspective

By giving attention to the following issues, relating to all forms of racism :

a) the economic basis of racism : the churches had become aware that racial exploitation and domination are commonly produced by and reflected in economic practices, including the operation of international monetary systems;

b) racism and sexism : it had become progressively more clear that women are victimized by racism even more than men are, most notably under the systems of migrant labour and apartheid. The links between racism and sexism, and the role of theology in perpetuating both, require more profound attention;

c) racial aspects of state repression : legislation on migration, citizenship crime and security together with its enforcement, will often be systematically oppressive in racial terms, either overtly or covertly; critical examination of these systems was needed, adopting the perspective of the racially oppressed;

d) land rights : ownership of and access to land was at the heart of the struggle for survival by racially oppressed groups in many continents;

e) a Charter of Rights : the PCR should work with other groups to secure through the United Nations, a Charter of Rights for oppressed and minority groups;

f) apartheid : new developments in the apartheid system, the intensifying struggle conducted by the racially oppressed and the continuing heretical claim made for apartheid as a defence of Christian civilization, all made the situation in South Africa and Namibia a particular priority for the attention of the churches;

g) theology : work already begun on racism in theology, on the different ways of doing theology and the dialogue between theologians from different regions should be further extended and supported;

h) education : the role of educational systems both in entrenching racist attitudes and values and in restricting human development needed to be exposed and corrected;

i) violence and non-violence : the Council had given proper and prolonged consideration to the question of violence and non-violence (e.g. in the resolution adopted by the Central Committee at Addis Ababa in 1971 and the report to the Central Committee in 1973 on "Violence and Non-violence in the Struggle for Social Justice"); it should give continued study to this matter, recognizing that violence is inherent in evil institutions and systems and as such has to be opposed, whenever possible by non-violent means.

In addressing these issues the PCR should identify and publicize models of positive achievements which contribute to racial justice and with which Christians can identify. Ways also needed to be found of restating that, while taking different forms, the liberation of the oppressor and of the oppressed where interdependent. Both were trapped in a spiral of fear and repression : oppressors must be liberated *from* blindness and guilt for a shared life in a more just and healthy community.

3. To take action within the WCC itself

a) WCC structures and practices : churches and their agencies had discovered a need to re-examine their own structures and institutional practices for possible racist elements; the same self-examination was therefore required of the WCC itself;

b) coordination with the WCC : many issues of racism related to and were addressed by other Sub-Units and Departments in the WCC (e.g. other Sub-Units within Unit II, CWME, Faith and Order, Programme for Theological Education, Office of Education, Women, Communication). The Staff Coordinating Group on Racism, which included representatives of all units and was moderated by the General Secretary, should act in assisting this cooperation.

STATEMENT FROM THE INTERNATIONAL CONSULTATION ON "THE CHURCHES' RESPONSE TO RACISM IN THE 1980s" IN THE NETHERLANDS (1980)

Every human being, created in the image of God, is a person for whom Christ has died. Racism, which is the use of a person's racial origins to determine the person's value, is an assault on *Christ's* values and rejection of *His* sacrifice. Wherever it appears, whether in the individual or in the collective, it is sin. It must be openly fought by all those who are on Christ's side, and by the Church as the designated vehicle and instrument of Christ's purpose in the world.

It is a matter of regret and for repentance that the churches have come so late to the recognition of this responsibility. They have been alerted to the struggle against racism, not by the appeals for solidarity from the victims of racism but by the spectacle of their defiant resistance. As demonstrated by the lengthening list of those who have given their lives, this struggle will continue — with or without the churches. In the struggle for every person's God-given freedom against the usurpers of that freedom, the churches must now be followers, in a field where they should have been pioneers at work on the frontiers.

Nevertheless, through the Programme to Combat Racism of the World Council of Churches, which goes along with other efforts in the area of human rights, the churches display some small recognition of their responsibility. The Programme is what St Paul would have described as an "arabon" — a small beginning, a deposit which is a guarantee of payment in full. So it is fitting that the WCC, having invited its member churches to consult at every level on how best they might combat racism within their own ranks and environs in the 1980s, should also call a consultation of this kind.

It is fitting also that in this consultation a prominent and important feature should be the patient listening to the voices of racially oppressed people themselves, recounting their experiences in their own way. So we were able to hear black people from South

Africa, Namibia and the USA, an Untouchable from India, an Aborigine from Australia, a Maori from New Zealand, a Tamil from Sri Lanka, a member of the Dene nation in Canada, a Native American, an Arab Palestinian from Israel, oppressed people from Guadeloupe, the Philippines, Haiti, the Netherlands and many others. Through their voices we were reminded of the plight of millions of oppressed castes, ethnic and racial groups.

We listened as well to other informed persons also engaged in the struggle against racism, who identified the specific issue which any group, including the churches, will have to tackle if their anti-racist stand is to be at all credible.

We discovered that certain themes surfaced in more than one area of the consultation. Among these was *the contribution that PCR had been able to make* over the ten years of its existence. Mentioned in this connection were the various projects (not always in the public eye) by which PCR had enabled racially oppressed people from different parts of the globe to overcome the barriers of language and distance, and to communicate face to face, thus strengthening one another in the struggle. Also mentioned was the prophetic nature of the *Special Fund* as demonstrated by support given to the liberation movements of Zimbabwe, Namibia and South Africa; and time and time again came the call that PCR should be strengthened and the Special Fund increased for its grants throughout the world.

But the contrast between this prophetic role and the *continuing racism in some church structures* was thrown into sharp relief. Too often the organization of the churches' life merely reflects their social environment, and members of society's weakest groups, including the racially oppressed, are also absent from leadership roles and the decision-making processes of the churches.

The need for the churches' uncompromised *witness against apartheid* was a recurring theme. In South Africa, there is added to the evil of dehumanizing people because God endowed them with black or brown skins, the blasphemy of the claim by the white oppressors that it is done to preserve Christian civilization. The churches' witness against apartheid cannot be limited to statements of abhorrence. Even while the consultation was in progress, news was being received of over sixty people shot down by South African police, to add to the numbers of those killed at Sharpeville, at Soweto, in Namibia, in police custody and in many other places, unreported and unrecorded.

Another recurring theme was the *economic basis of racism*. The dominant economic system of the world is one ordered to promote the self-interest, greed and values of the "white" world. This system exploits the natural and human resources of "Third World" peoples reducing them in the process to the status of impersonal units. Nowhere is this more clearly seen than in the phenomenon of the *so-called "migrant workers"*. Their very existence, without the security of citizenship or trade union membership and often without the supportive presence of their families, is tailored exclusively to the economic demands of an exploitative and soul-destroying system.

At the heart of the struggle by racially and culturally oppressed people for survival and liberation is the question of *land rights*. In many countries treaties are broken, expropriations made, nations of native people are forcibly removed from ancestral lands to make way for tourist developments, military bases, mining and so on. Since these outrages are executed by governments, or with the collusion of governments, the deprived peoples nearly always stand alone.

The justification for these and other genocidal practices is commonly given as development or "national security". *New doctrines of national security* have resulted in an intensification of racial discrimination and oppression. They are used to prevent changes in an unjust status quo and to maintain power structures. Racially oppressed and ethnic minorities seeking change in unjust laws and practices are often the victims of such measures, with banning, restrictions on movement and travel, detention without trial, pass laws, denial of the right of assembly and so on.

Strategic competition and conflict among great powers is reflected in *growing militarism*, increasingly sophisticated security systems and comprehensive computer-assisted surveillance. The doctrine of mutual deterrence fuels the arms race and has led to the placement of nuclear weapons which threaten all life on this planet. Conventional as well as high-technology weapons placed in client states are increasingly being used by them for the suppression of their own people and the domination of their neighbours.

The involvement of the churches at national and regional levels in the process of consultation has been most encouraging. We commend the findings of the regional consultations to the member churches for study and appropriate action at the local level.

In addition, this consultation was well served by a number of working groups. In forwarding these reports and recommendations to the Central Committee of the World Council of Churches and through it to the member churches, we call upon the churches to take note of the urgency of the situation and to be actively involved in the struggle against racism in the eighties in their national and regional situations and to support fully the programme of the WCC.

From among these recommendations we highlight the following :

1. We are strongly convinced that the 1980s demand the continuation and strengthening of the Programme to Combat Racism. It has played a significant role in the past decade in helping the churches to face the issue of racism and it is vital that it should remain an integral but distinct part of the work of the WCC. The Special Fund should continue as an active expression of solidarity with the struggle against racism, without change in the criteria for grants (see p. 98).

2. The churches, through PCR, should continue to give priority in Africa to Namibia and South Africa, while also lifting to a higher level of priority forms of racism in other parts of the world.

3. The World Council of Churches, through its member churches, should continue and intensify the educational process in matters of racism for the whole church community by :

a) maintaining the flow of information;
b) making it possible for church people to have an opportunity of listening personally to the racially oppressed;

c) making a task force available to visit member churches of the WCC and channel information, news and experience.

4. The WCC should urge member churches to undertake critical examination of the criminal justice systems (criminal laws and their enforcement) from the perspective of the racially oppressed and support efforts to remedy injustice.

5. The WCC should take up with the United Nations the urgent need to establish a Charter of Rights for oppressed minority groups and suitable instruments for monitoring its implementation effectively.

6. The WCC should seek to provide comprehensive legal advice and aid in countries where such help is not readily available to those involved in land struggles.

7. The PCR should pay attention to certain trends which will intensify in their impact on racism in the 1980s, such as :

a) the scramble for raw materials;
b) the oppression of minorities under the pressure of tightening economic circumstances;
c) increased secrecy on the part of power structures;
d) the persistence in some sectors of the Third World in seeking to copy the pattern of developments of the industrialized countries.

8. Oppressed racial goups should be encouraged to reflect theologically on their present and historical experience of oppression and to share this with the wider Church.

CRITERIA OF THE SPECIAL FUND TO COMBAT RACISM

1. The purpose of the organizations must not be in conflict with the general purposes of the WCC and its units, and the grants are to be used for humanitarian activities (i.e. social, health and educational purposes, legal aid, etc.).

2. The proceeds of the Fund shall be used to support organizations that combat racism, rather than welfare organizations that alleviate the effects of racism and which would normally be eligible for support from other units of the World Council of Churches.

3. (a) The focus of the grants should be on raising the level of awareness and on strengthening the organizational capability of the racially oppressed people. (b) In addition we recognize the need to support organizations that align themselves with the victims of racial injustice and pursue the same aobjectives.

4. The grants are made without control of the manner in which they are spent, and are intended as an expression of commitment by the PCR to the cause of economic, social and political justice which these organizations promote.

5. (a) The situation in Southern Africa is recognized as a priority due to the overt and intensive nature of white racism and the increasing awareness on the part of the oppressed in their struggle for liberation. (b) In the selection of other areas we have taken account of those places where the struggle is most intense and where a grant might make

a substantial contribution to the process of liberation; particularly where racial groups are in imminent danger of being physically or culturally exterminated. (c) In considering applications from organizations in countries of white and affluent majorities, we have taken note only of those where political involvement precludes help from other sources.

6. Grants should be made with due regard to where they can have the maximum effect: token grants should not be made unless there is a possibility of their eliciting a substantial response from other organizations.

STATEMENT FROM THE EXECUTIVE COMMITTEE, GENEVA (1981, 9-13 February)

Banks Doing Business in South Africa (p. 53)

The Executive Committee adopted the following criteria listed and described below as guidelines to the selection and use of banking deposit facilities and the continuation of banking relationships by the WCC.

a) **Bank maintains facilities in South Africa**

This includes the bank having a branch or representative office.

b) **Bank regularly appears as a "manager" of loans and/or bond issues to South Africa**

This means recognizing that banks play a leading role as "managers" as opposed to "participants", take a larger portion of the loans and/or bond issues and also receive a larger share of the fees in return.

c) **Bank has continued substantive lending since the events of Soweto — 1976**

1976 marked a clear statement by the African majority that it rejected apartheid. In turn, Soweto accelerated international concern about South Africa. Loans, private and public, since that time are generally done quietly and secretly with the lenders' awareness that they act in defiance of public pressure, moral opinion, and sometimes law.

d) **Bank grants loans having direct/indirect military purpose**

This involves loans or bonds going to the government itself, to the Defence Department or related bodies such as the South African Airways (SAA), the Strategic Oil Fund (SOF), the State Arms Procurement Agency (ARMSCOR) or the South African Railways and Harbours Authority (SARH).

e) **Bank makes loans which benefit the nuclear industry**

Many loans are made to ESCOM (the Electricity Supply Commission of South Africa) which wholly handles all nuclear energy questions in the country.

The Executive Committee *agreed* that relationships with banks may be continued if they have publicly stated a policy of no loans to the government of South Africa and its agencies, and openly maintain such a policy.

STATEMENT FROM THE EXECUTIVE COMMITTEE DRESDEN (1981, 14-16 August)

(pp. 17-18)

The Executive Committee accepted the following recommendations of the Finance Sub-Committee :

a) That WCC relations with the following banks be maintained :

Algemene Bank Nederland
Skandinaviska Enskilda Banken
Bankers Trust Company
Banque Scandinave en Suisse
Union Bank of Finland
Lloyds Bank Limited

b) That steps be taken to terminate WCC relations with the following banks :

Union Bank of Switzerland
Dresdner Bank
Swiss Bank Corporation

c) That WCC relations with the following banks be maintained pending the results of further dialogue with the banks concerned :

American Express Bank (Switzerland)
Banque Worms, Paris
Schroeder, Münchmeyer Hengst & Co
Banque Internationale pour l'Afrique Occidentale
Morgan Guaranty Trust Company, New York

d) That relationships may be established or extended with any or all of the following banks which are acceptable when compared to the criteria laid down, and which could serve as alternatives to those listed in (b) above :

Genossenschaftliche Zentralbank
Internationale Genossenschaftsbank
Algemene Bank Nederland, Geneva
Lloyds Bank Limited, Geneva

The Executive Committee also *accepted* the following recommendations of the Finance Sub-Committee :

— reference be made to the fact that these are the first major recommendations on banking relationships since 1974;

— that the decisions be seen as an integral part of consistent and continuing policy of the World Council of Churches over the past nine years;

— that the actions be seen as symbolic of the Council's full support for the liberation of South Africa from the system of racism embodied in apartheid;

— that the WCC believes it has no choice but to break its relations with banks which have provided satisfactory and, in one case, very long, financial services to the Council, but which are in contravention of the Council's long-stated position on bank loans to South Africa, and of the criteria which have been established.

STATEMENT FROM THE CENTRAL COMMITTEE DRESDEN, GDR (1981)

(pp. 75-76)

The Unit Committee considered and received the report of the PCR, a report on the proposed consultation on the churches' involvement in Southern Africa, and the separate report on a WCC team visit to Australia.

The Unit Committee had high praise for the report on the team visit to Australia pointing out that this report is important to the Aboriginal people because it puts their point of view before the public in a way never achieved before.

The Unit Committee wants to place on record the thanks of the WCC to the Aboriginal people and their organizations, as well as to the Australian Council of Churches for the hospitality and for all the help given to the WCC delegation.

On the request of the Unit Committee, the Central Committee *agreed* to endorse the recommendations included in the report, especially regarding international action, i.e. :

1. That the WCC, through its member churches, seek to direct international attention to the racism of the Queensland and Western Australian governments and the constitutional responsibilities of the Australian government. The forthcoming Commonwealth Heads of Government meeting and Commonwealth Games to be

held in Australia would provide opportunities for the churches to bring to the attention of Commonwealth countries, especially from Africa and Asia, the situation of Aborigines in Queensland;

2. That the WCC investigate the possibility of delegates from the International Commission of Jurists, the UN Human Rights Commission and Amnesty International making similar visits to Australian Aboriginal communities;

3. That the World Council of Churches' Commission on International Affairs and other sub-units be requested to inform member churches of the plight of Aboriginal communities in Australia.

On a proposal by Mr Bena-Silu, the Central Committee also *agreed* to request the General Secretary :

1. To forward the report of the World Council of Churches on the visit to the Aboriginal peoples to the Secretary General of the United Nations, and to the various regional organizations such as the OAU;

2. To report to the next Central Committee on the follow-up;

3. To write officially to the Australian Council of Churches to express gratitude of the Central Committee for the courageous attitude which it has adopted with regard to the struggle of Australian Aborigines for justice.

STATEMENT FROM THE CENTRAL COMMITTEE GENEVA (1982)

(pp. 70-73)

Land rights for indigenous people

The Central Committee *agreed* to adopt the statement.

On the recommendation of the Unit Committee, and in the light of the experiences, understandings and challenges contained in the statement, the Central Committee *agreed* to appeal to member churches to :

1. Listen to and learn from indigenous people in order to deepen Christian understanding of (and solidarity with) their legal rights, their political situation, their cultural achievements and aspirations, and their spiritual convictions;

2. Commit significant financial and human resources to the struggle of indigenous people for land rights;

3. Become politically involved on the side of indigenous peoples and join the struggle against those powers and principalities which seek to deny the land rights and human rights of indigenous people;

4. Support indigenous people struggling for land rights in their efforts to build linkage with other indigenous people around the world;

5. Act as a sign to the wider community of the churches' commitment to justice for indigenous people :

   a) To recognize the rightful claims of indigenous people and take steps to transfer land and property to them;

   b) to set up procedures to deal with the claims or demands of the indigenous people made upon the churches;

   c) to support the struggle of the people in their land claims through national and international courts of law;

6. Examine their investments in national and transnational corporations with a view to taking action to combat corporate policies affecting the lands of indigenous people;

7. Urge their governments to ratify and implement all relevant United Nations and other intergovernmental instruments for the protection of the rights of indigenous people;

8. Urge their governments to formulate adequate and effective national land rights legislation recognizing the collective property of the indigenous people.

The Central Committee *accepted* these recommendations.

The Central Committee *agreed* to :

1. Reaffirm that the issue of land rights for indigenous people should continue to be a priority for the work of the Programme to Combat Racism, as well as a concern of other sub-units of the WCC. The Programme to Combat Racism should involve other sub-units of the WCC in its work on this issue;

2. Request the Programme to Combat Racism in consultation with the Commission of the Churches on International Affairs to take appropriate actions in cooperation with other NGOs to gain international recognition for self-determination of the indigenous people on the lands to which they claim titles by indigenous traditions or treaties;

3. Welcome the creation by the United Nations of the working group on indigenous populations, and urge the United Nations, through its Commission on Human Rights, to give highest priority to the elaboration of appropriate international instruments for the protection and implementation of the rights of the indigenous peoples;

4. Request the Programme to Combat Racism to set up suitable mechanisms to examine the policies of international banks and other corporations which finance development projects affecting indigenous people and to take appropriate action to ensure that the rights of indigenous people are fully respected in such development programmes;

5. Strongly recommended that the issue of land rights for indigenous people be highlighted at the Vancouver Assembly and requests the Programme to Combat Racism staff, in consultation with the Assembly Preparation Committee, to make the necessary arrangements, including stimulating the imagination through highlighting the question of land rights and indigenous people by visual aids and other means such as personal testimonies at the Vancouver Assembly.

B. Consultation on churches' involvement in Southern Africa

1. The Unit Committee received with appreciation the report of this joint consultation which provides an excellent example of cooperation between two such bodies as the AACC and the WCC.

The Unit Committee requests the Central Committee to convey its expression of gratitude to the leadership of the AACC and the Christian Council of Zambia for their full cooperation in taking co-responsibility for the organization of this consultation. The Unit Committee is of the conviction that the consultation was held at a timely moment and the hope expressed that the recommendations contained in the report would help to strengthen the witness of the Christian church within South Africa and beyond.

2. The Unit Committee has urged the Assembly Preparations Committee to take seriously the recommendations made at the consultation regarding ways of highlighting Southern African issues at Vancouver, in particular :

— by arranging for liberation leaders to participate;

— by ensuring that Southern Africa concerns are fully on the Assembly agenda;

— by giving the liberation of South Africa and Namibia the highest visibility at the Assembly, e.g. through the provision of a special plenary session relating to Southern African issues;

— by providing suitable mechanisms for a steady flow of information to delegates.

3. The Unit Committee further recommends to the Central Committee that the General Secretary be requested to take necessary steps in following up the various recommendations which have implications for the WCC programmes, e.g. :

— the cooperation with AACC in the establishment of the proposed human rights resources office for Africa;

— the preparations for the formation of a communication network; and

— initiatives suggested in respect of theological education and a review of curricula in theological seminaries.

4. The Unit Committee also recommends that the Central Committee authorize the Programme to Combat Racism, in collaboration with the AACC, to prepare for the early publication of a full consultation report and assure its wide distribution to the churches and councils in the region and outside.

5. The Unit Committee finally urges the Central Committee to restate and re-emphasize its continuing commitment to the struggle for liberation in Southern Africa. This is particularly needed at this juncture in view of the accelerated militarization of South Africa and its attempts at destabilization of the countries in the region, and of the intensification of liberation struggles in South Africa and Namibia.

STATEMENTS FROM THE SIXTH ASSEMBLY OF THE WORLD COUNCIL OF CHURCHES VANCOUVER (1983)

REPORT OF ISSUE 6 : STRUGGLING FOR JUSTICE AND HUMAN DIGNITY
(p. 87)

Racism : The global reach of racism was highlighted in the 1980 WCC Consultation on "Churches Responding to Racism in the 1980s". Although the legalized apartheid system in South Africa is its most blatant and hideous form, racism rears its head in all parts of the world. Violence, even genocide against indigenous groups, has become endemic in many parts of the world.

Racism is often aggravated by international systems backed by powerful economic and military factors. Land rights claims of indigenous peoples are often rejected in the name of development and national security. Immigration policies and practices discriminate on the basis of race in many parts of Europe and North America. Education policies deny equality of opportunity and employment on the ground of race. In South Africa, so-called homelands have become dumping grounds for thousands deprived of their birthright and exiled from their homes in the interests of maintaining white supremacy. Resistance often results in banning, arbitrary arrest, detention without trial, and sometimes deaths under imprisonment. The proposed constitutional changes in South Africa promise to reinforce white rule, alienate blacks from one another and prevent their participation in shaping a common, just and peaceful society.

Some churches have begun to deepen their understanding of the root causes of contemporary racism. They also take some courageous action to confront the forces of racism nationally and globally. This has given new hope to the racially oppressed as they defiantly resist entrenched forces of racism. Racism is on the increase, but so are the struggles of the racially oppressed.

STATEMENT ON SOUTHERN AFRICA (pp. 151-156)

I. Preamble

1. Institutionalized racism in South Africa continues to be the central problem of justice and peace in the region, although there are several other situations in which human rights are infringed. We recall that in Nairobi (1975) the Assembly of the World Council of Churches declared "racism is a sin against God and against fellow human beings. It is contrary to the justice and the love of God revealed in Jesus Christ. It

84

destroys the human dignity of both the racist and the victim''. We would wish to add that it is a denial of the fullness of life which is Christ's gift to the world, for in him there is neither Greek nor Jew, there is neither slave nor free, there is neither male nor female, but all are one. Christ on his cross tore down the barriers of hostility which keep people apart (Eph. 2:14-16), thus establishing peace.

2. Apartheid raises barriers and denies the fullness of life in Christ. Christians and the churches are called in obedience to Jesus Christ the life of the world, and to maintain the integrity of the Church, to oppose apartheid in all its forms, to support those who struggle against this sinful system of injustice, and to denounce any theological justification of apartheid as a heretical perversion of the Gospel.

II. South Africa

3. The apartheid system perpetuates white minority rule at the cost of enormous suffering. Widespread and flagrant violations continue to be an everyday part of South African life. Restriction of movement, arbitrary arrests, detention without trial, torture and death have become an institutionalized way of intimidating black people and their supporters. Although a number of banning orders have recently been lifted, several people, including some leading Christians, continue to suffer from arbitrary banning orders.

4. Furthermore, large numbers of people are experiencing ongoing forced removals and relocation in resettlement camps, often in conditions of destitution, and violent government efforts to eliminate so-called "black spots" such as Driefontein as well as urban squatter areas such as Crossroads. The cost of these policies in terms of human suffering, the break-up of family and the creation of bitterness and despair is immense, and creates an extremely explosive climate.

5. In such a context a church which seeks to be the Church and to proclaim the liberating Gospel and the divine demand for justice cannot avoid a confrontation with the government. The Church did not seek a confrontation; it prayed that it would not happen. It continues to strive to be faithful to its own calling as it summons the state to fulfill the mandate which has been given to it by God.

6. In confessing the faith it is impossible in South Africa not to call for a fundamental change in the political, social and economic order of the country, not to speak for the oppressed and defend the rights and human dignity of the powerless. As the South African Council of Churches (SACC) has said, such a confession is "a cry from the heart, something we are obliged to do for the sake of the Gospel". As a consequence of the life and witness of the Christians and the churches, there is unrelenting pressure on them and the SACC, most recently shown in the activities of the Eloff Commission which appears to be an effort to muzzle and destroy the SACC.

7. Bantustan rule is in many instances as oppressive and arbitrary as that of white rule in the area, and has resulted in the proscription of churches and the systematic persecution of people. The willingness of some black leaders to accept this form of "independence" furthermore threatens to become the single most divisive and potent force militating against black solidarity and liberation in South Africa.

8. This Bantustan policy whereby blacks are being deprived of any kind of citizenship rights in other parts of South Africa and allocated to a variety of nominally independent "tribal homelands", has been followed by further constitutional proposals affecting Asians and "coloureds". According to these, Asians and "coloureds" would have specifically limited representation in a multicameral South Africa legislature with Asians and "coloured" ministers of state being appointed. It is necessary to indicate, however, that these proposals do not involve any sharing of political power. This will remain securely in white hands as constitutionally entrenched. These proposals are inherently racist and emphasize separation between the races rather than integration, and underscore the fact that blacks continue to be excluded entirely from the political process. In effect, these proposals, like the Bantustan policy, reaffirm the racist principles of apartheid.

II. Namibia

9. The remarkable courage of the Council of Churches in Namibia (CCN) in witnessing to Jesus Christ the life of the world, by standing with the oppressed, defending human rights and dignity and pressing for freedom and independence deserves wide recognition. The illegal South African occupation of the country is oppressive and generates many acts of terror against civilians. We endorse the open letter to the South African Prime Minister in January 1983 in which the Executive Committee of the CCN wrote :

"With no regard to the rights or the will of the people of Namibia, your Administrators-General continue a regime of draconian laws, proclamations and amendments which have destructive effects upon the people. We condemn the existence of all those laws that allow for the detention of people whitout recourse to a court of law, and call upon your government to charge or release all those who are detained under the so-called "security laws", including the survivors of Kassinga who are kept in a detention camp near Mariental. Further suffering and death are caused by curfews, conscription for military service and by brutal and unprovoked attacks on innocent people. Deportations, the refusal of passports and visas and the stifling of the true situation through bannings, also arouse our strong condemnation.

10. Negotiations for independence are stalled owing to obstruction by the South African government and its relentless refusal to recognize SWAPO as the legitimate representative of the Namibian people. This, together with the lethargy and apparently ineffectual influence of the Western Contact Group, motivated by short-term political and economic interests, only contributes to the prevailing conflict. Such a situation emphasizes the need for the Western Contact Group either to bring the South African government to the negotiation table or to disband. The insistence on linking the withdrawal of Cuban troops from Angola to Namibian independence is "an irrelevance" as was pointed out by the CCN. "The Cuban presence in the Sovereign State of Angola", CCN stated, "is not a threat to the Namibian people". Absolute priority must be given to both the termination of the illegal South African occupation of Namibia and to Namibian independence in accordance with United Nations Resolution 435.

IV. Destabilization

11. During the last decade South Africa, with the active collaboration of major Western powers and Israel, has been engaged in a massive military build-up which now includes nuclear weapons capability. This dangerous development poses a major threat to the peace and stability of the region. President Reagan's policy of "constructive engagement" and the recent loan of US dollars 1.25 billion to South Africa on very favourable terms by the International Monetary Fund are widely interpreted as signs of increased outside support for the South African regime which is pursuing a concerted policy of an "undeclared war against its neighbours" through destabilization and aggression.

12. A large area of Angola has been under South African occupation since 1981 and there have been numerous incursions deep into Angolan territory resulting in considerable loss of life. Subversives and military attacks have taken place in Mozambique and Lesotho and there is clear evidence of attempts at destabilization in Zimbabwe. This process of destabilization is clearly intended to perpetuate white dominance in the region.

V. Recommendations

13. The WCC Assembly, meeting in Vancouver, Canada, 24 July-10 August 1983 :

a) *reiterates* its conviction that apartheid stands condemned by the Gospel of Jesus Christ the life of the world, and that any theology which supports or condones it is heretical;

b) *expresses* its admiration and support for the prophetic and courageous stand for human dignity, justice and liberation taken by the South African Council of Churches and the Council of Churches in Namibia;

c) *calls* on the member churches to intensify their witness against apartheid and the continuing oppression in South Africa and Namibia, and to deepen their solidarity with those forces — including the liberation movements recognized by the UN — which oppose apartheid and racism, and struggle for liberation;

d) *assures* the white people of South Africa that its opposition is to apartheid as a system and that it loves them as brothers and sisters made in the image of God and prays that they may seek an end to apartheid and work for the establishment of a just and caring society;

e) *condemns* Bantustan "independence" as divisive and destructive force militating against black solidarity and liberation in South Africa;

f) *condemns* the new constitutional proposals in South Africa as fraudulent and racist because they do not provide for the real sharing of power and exclude blacks entirely from the political process;

g) *commends* the South African Council of Churches for rejecting the new constitutional proposals and draws the attention of the member churches to the full implications of the racist and divisive character of this proposed legislation;

h) recognizing the necessity for a society of justice in this subcontinent and re-affirming its abhorrence of all forms of violence, *urges* the member churches to do all in their powers to promote freedom of association, equality, democratic rights and the dismantling of apartheid as the essential ingredients of a political climate in which a national convention can be held;

i) *calls for* the independence of Namibia by the immediate implementation of UN Resolution 435 and requests the churches in the countries of the Western Contact Group to intensify pressure on their governments to give urgent and effective support;

j) *further deplores and condemns* attacks on neighbouring countries and efforts at destabilization by the South African government;

k) in view of the increasing number of refugees from this region, *calls upon* the member churches to use all appropriate means to render assistance to the people and also to work through existing refugee programmes;

l) *renews* its call to member churches to a disengagement from those institutions economically engaged in South Africa; *affirms* the need for mandatory and comprehensive sanctions and further *urges* governments which, through their fleets, are involved in transporting oil to South Africa, to take immediate steps, unilaterally or in cooperation with others, to bring an effective halt to the fuelling of apartheid;

m) *calls on* churches and Christian people throughout the world to express their support for and fellowship with the oppressed people of South Africa in prayer and every other appropriate way;

n) *calls on* member churches to discourage their people from emigrating to South Africa; and

o) *supports* the ongoing process of consultation and solidarity among the churches in Africa, in cooperation with the All Africa Conference of Churches, in their witness and struggle for liberation against apartheid and its consequences.

RESOLUTION ON THE RIGHTS OF THE ABORIGINAL PEOPLES OF CANADA (p. 164)

The World Council of Churches' Central Committee (August 1982) has called upon the member churches "to listen to and learn from indigenous people in order to deepen Christian understanding of (and solidarity with) their legal rights, their political situation, their cultural achievements and aspirations, and their spiritual convictions". At this Sixth Assembly in Vancouver, BC, Canada, we have been privileged to hear personal testimonies from and to share experiences with Aboriginal peoples of Canada. We give thanks to God for this witness and for the consistent support of the Canadian churches for these peoples' struggle to :

— gain recognition within Canada as distinct peoples uniquely attached to their traditional lands; and
— assert and gain respect for their human rights, including especially their fundamental rights to their land.

The Assembly expresses its solidarity with those struggles and, in the light of the First Ministers Conference on the Canadian Constitution on Aboriginal rights, title and treaty rights, urges the Federal and Provincial governments of Canada to recognize and enact Aboriginal title. Aboriginal rights and treaty rights in the Canadian Constitution in a manner and form acceptable to the Aboriginal peoples themselves. We further urge these governments to make no amendment or alteration to Aboriginal and treaty rights without the consent of the affected peoples.

The Assembly appeals to the member churches to support the Aboriginal peoples of Canada and the Canadian churches as they seek to achieve these ends; and requests the General Secretary to communicate this resolution to the appropriate governments and the Working Group on Indigenous Populations of the United Nations Commission on Human Rights.

STATEMENT FROM THE CENTRAL COMMITTEE, GENEVA (1984)

(pp. 33-36)

II. Southern Africa

One hundred years ago, the European powers gathered in the Berlin Conference to divide Africa among themselves. The anniversary of this event brings into sharp focus the continuing legacy of colonialism in that continent and particularly in Namibia. This country was among the first territories to be forcibly occupied by white rulers. It remains today a visible tragic symbol of an age characterized by genocide, exploitation, deprivation and the denial of the very humanity of conquered peoples.

Between the German occupation in 1884 and the takeover by South Africa in 1915, more than 100,000 Namibians were slaughtered. Still today, as international pressure has grown for a South African withdrawal, the bloodbath continues. The United Nations General Assembly in 1966 rescinded the South African mandate over South West Africa given by the League of Nations in 1920. Since then, an estimated 10,000 more Namibians, mostly civilians, have been killed as a result of South African military occupation.

The desperate plight of the people of Namibia has been of deep concern to the churches for decades. Namibians courageously resisted the occupation of their land from the outset. The Namibian churches have been in the forefront of the struggle for independence and human dignity. Today, through the Council of Churches in Namibia, churches representing more than 80% of the population have consistently and sacrificially opposed the racist South African rule. In their turn, churches around the world have expressed solidarity with Namibia. The World Council of Churches has supported the UN recognition of SWAPO (South West Africa People's Organization) as the sole, legitimate representative of the Namibian people. It has provided aid to the suffer-

89

ing through the churches, and humanitarian assistance to SWAPO. It has consistently promoted efforts toward a negotiated withdrawal of South Africa and the right to self-determination for the people of Namibia.

Namibia today can only be described as a military camp. An estimated 80,000 to 100,000 strong South African occupation force is desperately attempting to keep Namibia and its rich natural resources within the grasp of the *apartheid* system. Its methods of control have become ever more ruthless and cruel. Torture and assassination of randomly selected victims at the hands of groups like the notorious *Koevoet* (Crowbar) have become systematic.

Eighteen years ago the United Nations assumed direct responsibility for the Territory of Namibia in order to prepare its accession to independence. The moral and legal propriety of the Namibian people's right to self-determination has gained almost universal acceptance. As a means of achieving this goal, the United Nations Security Council adopted in 1978 Resolution 435. This provides for a supervised cease fire and elections under UN auspices.

Soon after, a five-power "Western Contact Group" (Canada, France, Federal Republic of Germany, United Kingdom, United States of America) was formed with the stated purpose of facilitating the implementation of this resolution. This process has slowed to a near standstill as more and more governments have been co-opted into the policy of "constructive engagement" with South Africa, and along with others have failed to apply comprehensive and mandatory sanctions aimed at ending South Africa's intransigence to Namibian independence. This has given encouragement to the apartheid regime which has engaged in a series of acts of diplomatic deception, in the hope of obtaining a form of "internal settlement" which would guarantee their continued hegemony over the land, resources and people of Namibia.

African states, especially those bordering on South Africa, have given sacrificial diplomatic and material support to Namibian refugees, and have attempted to mediate for a peaceful solution. In response, South Africa has engaged in intensive efforts to destroy African unity through military, economic, political and psychological pressures applied on a bilateral basis to independent States in Southern Africa.

In the same vein, Prime Minister Botha has recently visited some European States to seek their increased support and to attempt to bypass UN Security Council Resolution 435. On the occasion of that visit, the Executive Committee of the Council of Churches in Namibia sent an open letter to Christian churches in Europe and North America, which said : "In spite of the oft-repeated talk about peace, which South African leaders are presently parading to the world, we would testify that from our Christian point of view, no peace, or reconciliation built upon the unsure foundations of injustice and inequality can ever succeed".

"We thank you for your concern and care for us in the past", the letter concludes, "and now, as events move forward, we are more than ever conscious that your help under God will be increasingly necessary if the future of our land is to lead us to true peace, justice and the obtaining of our right to self-determination and freedom".

Giving thanks to God for the courageous struggle of the Namibian people and the witness of the Namibian churches, which encourages and strengthens churches around the world to confront injustice, threats to peace and denials of the integrity of Creation wherever they occur, the Central Committee of the World Council of Churches, meeting in Geneva, Switzerland, July 9-18, 1984 :

Reaffirms the Statement of Southern Africa adopted by the Sixth Assembly of the World Council of Churches in Vancouver (1983);

Expresses once again its solidarity with and deep appreciation for the courageous witness and leadership of the Council of Churches in Namibia and its member churches;

Deplores and condemns the attacks on and destruction of church property in the Territory and the arbitrary arrest and detention of church people by the South African occupation forces and their agents as a deliberate policy of intimidation;

Assures the churches in Namibia that the World Council of Churches' longstanding concern for justice and peace in their country will continue unabated in pursuit of the realization of the full rights of their people to self-determination and freedom;

Renews its support for the continuing process of consultation and solidarity among the churches in Africa in cooperation with the All Africa Conference of Churches in their witness and struggle for liberation against *apartheid* and its consequences;

Expresses particular appreciation for the insights provided by the National Conference of the South African Council of Churches held in Johannesburg, June 1984, and the May 1984 consultation in Lusaka of the Africa Christian Peace Conference; and

Appeals again to all member churches, especially those of Europe and North America to continue

a) to unmask and condemn South Africa's intensified campaign of deception through diplomacy;

b) to renew their commitment to the struggle for self-determination and independence for Namibia;

c) to press their own governments in cooperation with other groups opposing *apartheid* to implement UN Security Council Resolution 435, and other UN resolutions calling for mandatory sanctions which would bring South Africa to accept Namibia's right to self-determination;

d) to strengthen further the building up of the Body of Christ through continued spiritual and material support for the mission and witness of the Namibian churches engaged in the freedom struggle of their people, and to engage in constant and fervent prayer that the Namibian people shall soon be free.

STATEMENT FROM THE CENTRAL COMMITTEE GENEVA (1984)

(pp. 58-59)

The Unit Committee, having reviewed the programme proposals of PCR recommends that the Central Committee give approval to the general direction of the programme as well as the specific proposals of PCR.

The following suggestions are to be considered as the programme is developed. Recognizing that it is important for church leaders from Southern Africa engaged in the struggle against apartheid to visit other parts of the continent, it is suggested that ways of facilitating this process should be encouraged as well as team visit with Southern Africa as the focus.

The Unit Committee recommends that the Central Committee commend the document entitled *Recent Developments in Southern Africa* to member churches for study and action through the following resolution :

The WCC Central Committee, meeting in Geneva, 9-18 July 1984 :

Recalling the Vancouver Assembly Statement on Southern Africa which called on the churches "to intensify their witness against apartheid and continuing oppression in Southern Africa and Namibia, and to deepen their solidarity with those forces... which oppose apartheid and racism and which struggle for liberation",

Reaffirming the WCC's longstanding commitment to take all appropriate steps to support the struggle for lasting justice and liberation in the region,

Draws the attention of the churches to the following recent developments :

1. The recent accords by South Africa with Mozambique and Angola have created the false, misleading and dangerous impression that South Africa has now seriously embarked on a policy of establishing peace in the region and in South Africa itself;

2. The Constitutional Proposals are fraudulent and racist because they do not provide for the real sharing of power and exclude blacks entirely from the political process;

3. South African blacks continue to suffer from oppression, poverty, harassment, brutality and cruelty of the pass laws while apartheid remains an instrument of economic exploitation;

4. The forced removals of people from the "black spots" cause even greater hardship among the black population and tear families apart;

5. Churches inside South Africa have been critical of these developments and have urged the ecumenical community to intensify all its efforts to oppose apartheid, the root of these injustices;

6. There are significant manifestations of the unity and strength of the black people inside South Africa through new movements for justice and dignity.

92

The Central Committee *accepted* these recommendations.

Note : In the Report on Unit II, it is recalled that the Assembly asked the PCR "to build up a network of black youth from the USA, Africa, the Caribbean, Latin America and the Pacific".

It is the feeling of the Central Committee that black youth in Europe should be added to this list.

STATEMENTS FROM THE CENTRAL COMMITTEE OF THE WORLD COUNCIL OF CHURCHES BUENOS AIRES, ARGENTINA, JULY-AUGUST 1985

MEMORANDUM ON SOUTHERN AFRICA (Appendix V, p. 109)

1. The Executive Committee of the South African Council of Churches (SACC) adopted on 16 April 1985 a "Call for A Day of Prayer for the end to unjust rule in South Africa". The accompanying document stated :

> "We now pray that God will replace the present structures of oppression with ones that are just and remove those in power who persist in defying His laws, installing in their place leaders who will govern with justice and mercy... We pray that God's rule may be established in this land. We pledge ourselves to work for that day, knowing that this rule is good news to the poor because the captives will be released, the blind healed, the oppressed set at liberty, and the acceptable year of the Lord proclaimed."

2. The SACC in invoking the words of the Prophet Isaiah once again challenges the people of South Africa and the world with the vision of God's justice. We are called upon, with prayer, to translate that vision into reality through our actions to promote the creation of a just multiracial society, in which violence and hostility between the peoples of Southern Africa give way to peace.

The State of Emergency

3. The declaration of a state of emergency in 36 magisterial districts of South Africa by the South African government on 20 July 1985 represents a further escalation of the oppression and violence carried out by the government against its own people and those of neighbouring lands in the region, like Botswana, Lesotho, Angola and Mozambique, and not least in Namibia whose illegal occupation by South Africa continues unabated. Desparate to sustain the unsustainable, the government confers on itself powers over the liberty and movement of persons, and controls over property, services and information, which can only multiply the sufferings of the people and set back still further just and non-violent solutions. The rule of law in South Africa, at the best of times tenuous, has now effectively ceased to exist for large sections of the country's population.

4. The response of the SACC to this new situation has been to continue to bear courageous witness to the Gospel of Christ. In the face of the growing violence of which it had consistently warned, and for the avoidance of which it had long prayed and worked, the SACC's message to the South African government was clear and must be echoed here :

"The awful blood-bath long prophesied is upon us... heed our urgent call by releasing all political prisoners, by allowing the exiles to return, by listening to the voice of the authentic believers, only then will peace with justice come to our land."

Economic Pressure on Southern Africa

5. Christians outside South Africa, in the face of a continuing spiral of violence, have an inescapable responsibility for the current and future state of affairs. An ever-increasing militarization and the nuclear capability of South Africa deserve mention. A non-violent resolution to the situation in South Africa is only possible with the active participation and support of those of us outside that country for measures to maximize the economic pressure on the South African government to abandon its intransigent refusal to come to terms with the overwhelming majority of its population, and to recognize their right to participate in the creation of a just multiracial society in South Africa.

6. Recognition must be given to the activities of many — Christians and non-Christians together — who have promoted campaigns in which many churches have played a significant part in raising the issues of disinvestment, an end to bank loans, and other measures of economic and military boycott and disengagement from South Africa. The success of these campaigns in conscientizing the world community and in bringing effective pressure to bear on an economy bloated by the exploitation of blacks in South Africa is critical to the non-violent resolution of the conflict. At the same time that economic pressure is brought to bear on South Africa, economic aid must be increased to the front-line states in order to help them decrease their economic ties to South Africa.

7. The United States, South Africa's largest trading partner, holding a quarter of foreign investment (direct and indirect) in that country, has seen the work of many churches, anti-apartheid groups and the Free South Africa Movement result in the passing by the House of Representatives of a package of sanctions including a ban on the sale of Kruger rands, halt of nuclear exports, sale of computers and restrictions on bank loans. The campaign against Kruger rands has seen success in both Europe and North America. Sweden, Denmark and Norway all took legislative measures in early 1985 to step up the level of economic pressure by those countries on South Africa. The United States and Great Britain refrained from using their veto against a French resolution in the UN Security Council in response to the state of emergency calling for voluntary sanctions against South Africa. These are significant contributions, but much remains to be done if such pressure is to reflect itself in a change of policy by the South African government.

8. The SACC answered those who doubt the wisdom of economic sanctions at its National Conference in June 1985. Having reiterated its earlier statement that foreign

investment and loans have been used to support prevailing patterns of power and privilege in South Africa, the Conference resolved :

"To express our belief that disinvestment and similar economic measures are now called for as a peaceful and effective means of putting pressure on the South African government to bring about those fundamental changes this country needs;

"To ask our partner churches in other countries to continue with their efforts to identify and promote effective pressures to influence the situation in South Africa towards achieving justice and peace in this country and minimizing the violence of the conflict."

9. The authority of the SACC in making this call has been enhanced and underpinned by its increased and important links with the trade union movement in South Africa. These give the lie to the repeated statements by the South African government that economic sanctions are contrary to the wishes and interests of the majority of black workers in South Africa, and assertion which is in any event undermined by the government's own stated intention to expel black migrant workers from South Africa in retaliation for the stepping up of economic measures against South Africa. They reveal by this threat a total lack of concern for the working population of South Africa.

The Failure of "Constructive Engagement"

10. The US policy of "constructive engagement" is seen to be totally ineffective in constraining the government of South Africa in its internal repression and also in limiting its destabilizing influence throughout the South African region. In addition, the US and other governments such as those of the Federal Republic of Germany, France and the United Kingdom which supported "constructive engagement", find such a policy difficult to sustain both domestically and internationally.

11. In South Africa the government has responded to the growing resistance by arresting leaders of the UDF, AZAPO and some trade unions, accusing them of "high treason". Seeking to divide and confuse its opposition, the government's security forces have actively promoted a campaign of murder and violence within the black townships. These actions, aimed at removing authentic and credible leadership whilst at the same time fermenting inter-communal violence, the murder of blacks by blacks — courageously condemned by Bishop Desmond Tutu — can only lead to a deterioration of the situation and are to be deplored.

Namibia

12. Namibia remains a constant reminder that the violence and oppression the South African government extends beyond its own territory and presents a threat to peace and justice in the whole region. The South African government seeks to cloak its activities in Namibia with a spurious legitimacy by installing in Windhoek on 17 June 1985 an Interim Government composed of members of the Multi-Party Conference. The Council of Churches in Namibia (CCN), expressing its dismay at these developments, stated that the Multi-Party Conference "has no democratic electoral mandate or support from the Namibian people". With the major portfolios like Defence, Security, Finance and Foreign Affairs in the hands of the government of Pretoria, the "Interim Government"

is a transparent attempt to circumvent international law and public opinion. The South African government's intention is clearly to continue to exclude SWAPO, the sole and legitimate representative of the Namibian people, from the government of Namibia, making it a "client state" with national independence, but totally subservient to the interests of the South African government. This development has taken place within the context of increased military activity both within Namibia and in Angola, the forced registration of all adults males, including priests, for military service and growing internal oppression. The Western Contact Group has shown itself incapable of securing the withdrawal of South Africa from Namibia and the independence of that country in accordance with UN Resolution 435, correctly described by the CCN as "the only basis for a peaceful solution".

The Youth of Southern Africa

13. The young people of Southern Africa are amongst the most numerous victims of apartheid and number amongst the strongest and most active of its opponents. They feature prominently in the lists of those missing, dead, imprisoned, and those to stand trial. They have no future under apartheid but continued oppression and exploitation. They are denied the right to develop into adulthood with the hope of a life in which they can explore the fullness of their human potential.

14. The declaration by the UN of 1985 as the International Year of Youth requires, if it is to have any meaning in the context of Southern Africa, that the struggle of youth in Southern Africa for peace and justice receive greater recognition and solidarity from the community of world youth. The SACC has accordingly called for the launching of a World Youth Campaign, including amongst other things prayer, support for the sanctions and disinvestment movement, and organized cultural and economic boycott and worldwide "sit-ins" at South African embassies by the youth of the world.

Christian Concern and Action

14. The future of these young people and Southern Africa as a whole is a matter of utmost concern for the churches and for Christians throughout the world. The option for a non-violent solution remains open, but requires, if it is to be translated into something other than a pious hope amidst increasing violence, a focusing of our prayers and a concentration of our efforts around actions designed to promote this objective. God's justice requires our hand in work and prayer if His will is to be done in Southern Africa.

MEMORANDUM AND RECOMMENDATIONS ON SOUTHERN AFRICA
(p. 26-27)

The Central Committee of the World Council of Churches, meeting in Buenos Aires, Argentina, 28 July-8 August 1985 :

a) *reiterates* the conviction stated by the Sixth Assembly that "apartheid stands condemned by the Gospel of Jesus Christ and that any theology which supports it or condones it is heretical";

b) *expresses* its continued admiration and support for the prophetic and courageous stand of the SACC and the CCN for human dignity, justice and liberation in Southern Africa;

c) *calls* on member churches to join with the SACC in prayer for "the end of unjust rule in South Africa", and to uphold the work of the SACC and CCN in prayer and thanksgiving for their continued witness to the Gospel of Christ;

d) *condemns* the declaration of a state of emergency by the South African government as an escalation of violence and oppression against the South African peoples and a further obstacle to a non-violent resolution of conflict between the peoples of South Africa;

e) *supports* the SACC in calling on the South African government for an end to the state of emergency, the release of all political prisoners, to allow the return of exiles and to heed the voice of the authentic leaders of the South African peoples;

f) *condemns* the installation of an Interim Government in Namibia as an attempt to bypass UN Resolution 435, which it *reaffirms* as the only basis for peace and the genuine independence of Namibia, and *expresses* its support for SWAPO as the authentic representative of the people of Namibia;

g) *calls* on member churches of the WCC to share with the General Secretariat in Geneva the policies developed and actions taken in response to the various calls of the WCC for disinvestment, an end to bank loans to South Africa and to military/nuclear collaboration with South Africa, before the next meeting of the Central Committee;

h) *expresses* its admiration and support for action already taken throughout the world, but particularly in the US, Scandinavia and the Netherlands, to bring pressure to bear on the South African government through economic and other measures, and *calls* on the churches to step up their support and activities in this regard and in furtherance of promoting their countries' compliance with recent UN resolutions on South Africa as an essential prerequisite of a non-violent solution to the problems of Southern Africa;

i) *commends* the courageous action of the SACC in calling for economic sanctions against South Africa and its valuable work with the trade union movement in South Africa on this issue, *calling* on member churches likewise to work with the trade union movements of their own countries to enhance the development of effective economic measures against South Africa;

j) *recognizes* the struggle and suffering of youth in Southern Africa and joins with the SACC in calling for a world youth campaign as part of the UN Year for Youth, and *calls* on member churches to work with local youth organizations to promote solidarity with the youth of Southern Africa;

k) *reiterates* its support for the ongoing process of consultation and solidarity among the churches in Africa, in cooperation with the All Africa Conference of Churches, in their witness and struggle for liberation against apartheid and its consequences particularly for neighbouring states in the region;

l) *calls* on churches and Christian people throughout the world to express their support for and fellowship with the oppressed people of Southern Africa generally and their liberation movements, the victims of the state of emergency and "treason" trials, in particular through prayer and in other manifestations of concern and solidarity;

m) *assures* again the white people of South Africa that its concern and love extends to them also as brothers and sisters made in the image of God and *prays* that they may cooperate in seeking an end to apartheid and the establishment of a just and caring society.

SACC :   South African Council of Churches
CCN :   Council of Churches in Namibia
SWAPO : South-West Africa People's Organization
UDF :   United Democratic Front
AACC :   All Africa Conference of Churches
AZAPO : Azanian People's Organization

SELECTIVE RECENT LITERATURE
ON RACISM FOR FURTHER READING

"Ecumenical Statements on Race Relations" (1965) and Elisabeth Adler's book : "A Small Beginning" (1974) contain bibliographies of earlier literature on racism.

WCC DOCUMENTS

ADLER, Elisabeth. *A Small Beginning. An Assessment of the First Five Years of the Programme to Combat Racism.* Geneva : WCC, 1974.
Describes the historical context of the PCR, its policy and programme, the participation of the churches in the PCR and attempts a first critical evaluation. The appendices contain : highlights in the history of racism and the fight against it, a chronology of the PCR, plan for an Ecumenical Programme to Combat Racism (the Canterbury mandate), grants made from 1970-1974, list of publications on racism and contributions towards the Special Fund 1970-1973.

ALLISON, Caroline. *It's like holding the key to your own jail. Women in Namibia.* Geneva : WCC, 1986.
Gives a view of the day-to-day life and struggle of Namibian women.

BARNABY, Frank. *Nuclear Proliferation and the South African Threat.* Geneva : WCC, CCIA and PCR, 1977 (E and F).
A careful analysis of complex issues by the Director of the Stockholm International Peace Research Institute. The nuclear development of South Africa is particularly disturbing because of the special political situation in that country and the threat it poses to the area.

"DEPLACEMENTS de Population". Rapport des Eglises sur les déportations de populations en Afrique du Sud, PCR 1984.
This is a translation of the report of the South African Council of Churches and the Roman Catholic Bishop's Conference of Southern Africa on Forced Removals in South Africa.

"ECUMENICAL Statements on Race Relations. Development of Ecumenical Thought on Race Relations 1937-1964". Geneva : WCC, 1965.
Already referred to in the Preface of this booklet. It includes as a first statement a declaration from the Oxford Conference, 1937 and a bibliography of earlier literature on racism until 1964.

"FUELLING Apartheid : Shell and the Military", published by CCSA, Kairos, CIIR and PCR in 1984.
This report describes Shell's involvement in South Africa.

HEUVEL, Albert van den. *Shalom and Combat. A personal Struggle Against Racism.* Geneva : WCC, 1979 (The Risk Book Series).
Mixed with the autobiography is a penetrating analysis of how the ecumenical movement has slowly come to grips with the evil of racism. Descriptions of the controversy around the WCC's Special Fund to Combat Racism provide a backdrop to what is essentially a personal confession.

"JUSTICE for Aboriginal Australians". Report of the World Council of Churches team visit to the Aborigines June 15 to July 3, 1981. Geneva : WCC, Programme to Combat Racism, 1981.
The report covers the concerns of the Aborigines like land rights, mining, health, housing. Several recommendations for actions are made.

KAMEETA, Zephania. *Why, O Lord. Psalms and sermons from Namibia.* Geneva : WCC, 1986 (The Risk Book Series).
These writings are born out of the reality of suffering and the longing for liberation. Their background is that of apartheid and the oppressive structures based on it.

LUCKHARDT, Ken & WALL, Brenda. *Working for Freedom. Black Trade Union Development in South Africa Throughout the 1970s.* Geneva : WCC, Programme to Combat Racism, 1981.
After giving a background to the present situation, the major part of the book puts the workers' struggles in an analytical perspective, demonstrating their significance in current South African realities.

MILITZ, Eva. *Bank Loans to South Africa, Mid-1982 to End 1984.* Geneva : WCC, 1985.
Statistics of bank loans, including an explanatory introduction and background information.

"NO Last Frontier". In : RISK, vol. 13, No. 2, 1977.
Deals with the Dene nation and the struggle of Canada's internal colony for self-determination. The decisions to be taken are not simply about northern pipelines but about the protection of the northern people and its environment.

"PCR INFORMATION. Reports and Background Papers". Geneva : WCC, Programme to Combat Racism, appears approximately four times per year. The following issues have been published :

No. 1/1979 — WCC Central Committee Resolutions on PCR, Kingston, Jamaica, January 1-11, 1979
— Extracts of Report by the General Secretary to the Central Committee

No. 2/1979 — Namibia, Recent Developments

No. 3/1979 — Bank Loans and Investments in Southern Africa : A survey of actions taken by churches and groups in relation to WCC policies
— Grants from the Special Fund 1979

No. 4/1980 — Racism and the Unity of the Church
— Notes on a Theology for Combating Racism
— Violence and Non-violence — Resuming the debate
— Violence in the Struggle Against Racism in South Africa
— The Special Fund to Combat Racism — A discussion paper

No. 5-9/1980 — "Churches Responding to Racism in the 1980s".
Preparatory documents and reports of the national and regional consultation leading to the World Consultation on Racism which took place in Noordwÿkerhout, the Netherlands, 16-21 June 1980. A special edition of PCR Information gives the report of the World Consultation.

No. 10/1980 — Robert Mugabe : Talk at the Church Center for the U.N., New York, August 1980
— Canaan Banana : Opening Address to the Clergy Revival Conference, Salisbury, September 1980
— Racism and Rumours of Racism. Toward a framework for thinking about racial domination in the USA in the 80s
— Africa on the Way to a New International Information Order

No. 11/1981 — Namibia — Recent Developments
James Baldwin : Notes on the House of Bondage. Announcements. Reviews

No. 12/1981 — South Africa : Bishop Desmond Tutu's Address to the British Council of Churches (March 1981)
— Brazil — Manaos : Conference on Indigenous Peoples
— USA : Racism in the Atlanta Murders. Announcements. Reviews

No. 13/1981 — NGO Conference on Indigenous People and the Land
— Guaymi People Defending their Land
— The Yanomami Indians Need Support in the Defence of their Traditional Land
— Transnational Corporations and Indigenous People
— Announcements

Special Issue — Bricks in the Wall. An update on foreign bank involvement in South
(March 1981)   Africa. Background paper by Beate Klein

No. 15/1982 — Organized, Racial Violence — New Trends. Features, incl. e.g. :
— The KKK in the USA
— Britain and the case for self-defence
— Is Brazil really a racial democracy ?
— Genocide in Guatemala
— The Tamil Scapegoat : The Roots of Racism in Sri Lanka
— Book Reviews — Announcements
— New Resources

No. 16/1983 — Land Rights for Indigenous People, incl. statements and declara-
tions on the subject from different organizations
— Selected Resources on Land Rights
— Selected Indian Organizations
— Announcements (E and S)

Special Issue — Report of the Consultation on "The Churches' Involvement in
(July 1983)   Southern Africa", held in Mindolo Ecumenical Centre Kitwe,
Zambia, 24-28 May 1982

No. 18/1984 — Assembly 1983
— Statements and Speeches
— News Items (USA, South Africa)
— Announcements

No. 19/1985 — Women under Racism
— Articles and Reports
— Book Reviews and Announcements
— News Items

No. 20/1985 — Racism in Western Europe, features :
— Migrant workers, black communities and Gypsies
— News Items
— Book Reviews

No. 21/1985 — Southern Africa : The Continuing Crisis, features :
— Recent Developments in Southern Africa
— The United Democratic Front
— News on Bishop Desmond Tutu, Rev. Allan Boesak and Rev.
Beyers Naude and the SACC
— Statements of Churches on Southern Africa
— Announcements of new books
— News Items
— Special Fund Grants 1984

Special Issue — Challenge to the Church.
(Nov. 1985)   A Theological Comment on the Political Crisis in South Africa —
The Kairos Document.

102

"RACISM in Children's and School Textbooks". Geneva : WCC, Programme to Combat Racism — Office of Education, 1979.
A report based on the documents and discussion of the First Workshop on "Racism in Children's and School Textbooks", at the Evangelische Akademie Arnoldshain, FRG, 13-18 October, 1978.

"RACISM in Theology. Theology Against Racism". Geneva : WCC. 1975.
Report of a Consultation organized by the Commission of Faith and Order and the Programme to Combat Racism dealing with the Christian witness against racism : collective repentance in corporate action and reflection; the struggle against racism and the search for a just society; the role of the church : discipleship and disciplined life; and considerations and recommendations for further action.

"THE SITUATION of the Indians in South America. Contributions to the study of Inter-Ethnic Conflict in the Non-Andean Regions of South America". Ed. by W. Dostal. Geneva : WCC, 1972.
A report and documents of a Symposium on inter-ethnic conflict in South America, organized by the Ethnology Department of the University of Bern (Switzerland) and sponsored by the WCC Programme to Combat Racism and the Commission of the Churches on International Affairs, Bridgetown, Barbados, 25-30 January, 1971.

SJOLLEMA, Baldwin. *Isolating Apartheid. Western Collaboration with South Africa : Policy Decisions by the World Council of Churches and Church Responses.* Geneva : WCC, 1982.
The first part of the book provides a detailed information on the facts of apartheid in South Africa. It exposes how the Western nations, in a variety of ways, aid and abet the apartheid regime in that nation. The second part gives an account of what the WCC and some of its member churches and councils have done in recent years in opposing apartheid.

ROGERS, Barbara. *Race : No Peace Without Justice. Churches Confront the Mounting Racism in the 1980s.*
The book gives a critical account of the WCC/PCR World Consultation in June 1980.

In 1984, PCR also published a new flyer on its work (E + G).

OTHER RECENT LITERATURE

"APARTHEID. The Facts" by the International Defence and Aid Fund. London : IDAF, 1983.
A comprehensive handbook on the current situation in South Africa. Brings together detailed, up-to-date information in an easily accessible form, much of it with the help of maps, graphs and photos.

"A BLACK Christian in Southern Africa" by a Daystar Reporter. Lusaka : Daystar Publications, 1976.
Tells the story of S.E.M. Pheko's jail and Christian experiences in South Africa, Rhodesia and Mozambique. When editing a Christian magazine his role changed from preaching Christ to defending the liberation struggle of the African people against colonialism and racism.

"BLACK Theology — A Documentary History, 1966-1979". Ed. by Gayraud S. Wilmore and James H. Cone. Maryknoll, NY : Orbis Books, 1979.
This book is an authoritative interpretation of black theology as a major contemporary theological, religious, social and political movement. It contains many contributions on civil rights and black power, the attack on white religion, black theology and the response of white theologians, black theology and black women, black theology and Third World theologies.

BOESAK, Allan A. *Farewell to Innocence. A Socio-Ethical Study on Black Theology and Black Power.* Maryknoll, NY : Orbis Books, 1977.
Written by a South African theologian out of the anguish of the black experience in his nation. "Until now", the author asserts, "the Christian Church had chosen to move through history with a bland kind of innocence, hiding the painful truths (of oppression and the need for liberation of the black) behind a façade of myths and the real or imagined anxieties."

BOESAK, Allan A. *Black and Reformed. Apartheid, Liberation and the Calvinist Tradition.* Ed. by Leonard Sweetman. Maryknoll, NY : Orbis Books, 1984.
This book represents a collection of addresses that Allan Boesak delivered between 1974 and 1983 to various assemblies, including to black citizens of South Africa as they were organizing themselves into a political movement. The voice is that of Allan Boesak, but the pulse is that of South Africa's suffering black people.

CARNE, Derek. *Land Rights. A Christian Perspective.* Prepared by the Task Force on Land Rights for Aboriginal People. Established by Australian Council of Churches Catholic Commission for Justice and Peace. Chippendale : Alternative Publishing Cooperative, 1980.
In general, the following themes are dealt with : land rights and Aboriginal culture, land rights and European culture, land rights and the Church.

CONE, James H. *For my People. Black Theology and the Black Church.* Maryknoll, NY : Orbis Books, 1984.
This book examines black theology between 1966 and 1984 and makes a critical assessment of its origin and its development in order to chart the course of its future. It seeks to give a theological interpretation of the civil rights movement and of other race-related issues stemming from it.

DAVIS, James H. and Woodie W. *Racial Transition in the Church.* Nashville : Abingdon, 1980.
The result of six years of research in twenty cities and among hundreds of congregations, this book studies the experiences of churches in racial transition and plots a course for the future.

DESMOND, Cosmas. *Christians or Capitalists. Christianity and Politics in South Africa.* London : Bowerdean Press, 1978.
The author's thesis is that the roots of injustice in South Africa are to be found, not in racism but in the capitalist economic system, which as he convincingly shows, has exploited racism for the purpose of maintaining power and prosperity. It is axiomatic, therefore, that God both in history and in His Son has shown himself to be on the side of the poor and the exploited.

"DIVESTMENT For South Africa : An Investment in Hope". New York : Committee on Mission Responsibility Through Investment, 1985.
Contains the report and recommendations on South Africa divestment approved by the 197th General Assembly (1985); and the report and recommendations on divestment as an ethical strategy approved by the 196th General Assembly (1984).

HECKEL, Roger. *The Struggle Against Racism. Some Contributions of the Church.* Vatican City : Justitia et Pax, 1979.
A publication sponsored by the Pontifical Commission "Justitia et Pax" dealing with "the decade of action to combat racism and racial discrimination (1973-1983)" and the Holy See's participation in some more contingent aspects of the common human effort.

HODGSON, Peter C. *Children of Freedom. Black Liberation in Christian Perspective.* Philadelphia : Fortress Press, 1974.
The book is a serious attempt to respond to James Cone's charge that "no white theologian has ever taken the oppression of black people as a point of departure for analyzing God's activity in contemporary America."

HOLDEN, Tony. *People, Churches and Multi-Racial Projects. An Account of English Methodism's Response to Plural Britain.* London : The Methodist Church, 1985.
This report is an account of how one British church has responded to Britain becoming multi-ethnic, multi-racial and multi-faith. Also includes reflections and recommendations for action.

KNIGHT, Derrick. *Beyond the Pale. The Christian Political Fringe.* Lancashire : Caraf, 1982.
The author brings to light significant information on the Christian and political groups currently leading a crusade against the World Council of Churches and reveals their connections with extreme right-wing political movements. The book explores the work of the South African Information Department and the reasons for the campaign.

MIDDLETON, M.R. *The Black Church vs. the System.* New York : Vantage Press, 1976.
A study of the First Congregational Church of Atlanta, Georgia — a high status church located in a decaying, downtown area of the city. The membership of the church consistently declined and a significant proportion moved to residential districts rated "high".

PIYADASA, L. *Sri Lanka : The Holocaust and After.* London : Marram Books, 1984. This book shows why the racist pogroms, the context in which they occurred, and the indications of further violence, as well as the demand of many Tamils for a separate state, demand a more penetrating scrutiny of Sri Lankan society.

RADER, William. *The Church and Racial Hostility. A History of Interpretation of Ephesians* 2:11-22. Tübingen : Mohr, 1978.
A study prompted by the racial problem in the USA, and particularly in the inner city of Cincinnati. It is based on the thesis that the uniting of Jew and Gentile in the early life of the Church has significance for the understanding of the Church today.

RICHARDSON, Neville. *The World Council of Churches and Race Relations : 1960-1969.* Bern : H. Lang, 1977 (Studies in the Intercultural History of Christianity, vol. 9).
The chapters are titled : The Matrix of World Council Thought on Race Relations; Policy and Action. — I : Contact, Consultation and Statement; New Directions in the Social Thought of the World Council of Churches; Policy and Action. — II : Confrontation and Conflict; Conclusion.

ROBERTS, James Deotis. *Black Theology. Today-Liberation and Contextualisation.* New York and Toronto : Edwin Mellen Press, 1983 (Toronto Studies in Theology, vol. 12).
This is a collection of essays on the hermeneutics and method of black theology, oppression and liberation in world history, the impact of the black church, the unfinished agenda of civil rights, the priestly and prophetic dimensions of black spirituality, the black church and family and the power structure.

SERFONTEIN, J.H.P. *Apartheid Change and the NG Kerk.* Emmarentia : Taurus, 1982.
J.H.P. Serfontein has increasingly established himself as an authority on developments in the Afrikaans churches, and especially in the NG Kerk. In this book he discusses the events in and around the NGK in the period October 1978 to May 1982, analysing the debate inside the NGK. He comes to the conclusion that "there are no signs of real, fundamental change in the policies of either the government and the NGK".

"SOUTH AFRICA in the 1980s" by the Catholic Institute for International Relations. London : CIIR, first published in 1980.
Since the publication of "South Africa in the 1980s", the CIIR has published three updates. They cover topics like "economy", "the state's strategy", "resistance", "the churches" and South African politics in Southern Africa.

"THE EXTREME RIGHT in Europe and the United States". Ed. drs. Vera Ebels-Dolanová. Amsterdam : Anne Frank Foundation, 1985.
This book is based on the proceedings of an international seminar, hold by the Foundation, the information provided by the participants and on research conducted by the organisation.

TUTU, Desmond. *Crying in the Wilderness.* Ed. and introduced by John Webster. London & Oxford : Mowbray, 1982.
This collection of the Winner of the Peace Nobel prize for 1984, Bishop Tutu's sermons,

speeches, articles and press statements documents a lively two-and-half years in the life of the South African Council of Churches. It goes from Bishop Tutu's appointment as General Secretary on 1 March 1978 to the abortive meeting between the SACC and the South African then-Prime Minister and government in August 1980.

WEST, Cornel. *Prophesy Deliverance ! An Afro-American Revolutionary Christianity.* Philadelphia : Westminster Press, 1982.
The author discusses the Afro-American experience in the light of the social and intellectual currents that shaped American culture, and examines the relationship of African, American and European elements in this experience. He looks at the genealogy and cultural roots of racism, providing a theoretical understanding of four traditional black responses to the doctrine of white supremacy.

YOSHINO, I. Roger & MURAKOSHI, Sueo. *The Invisible Visible Minority. Japan's Burakumin.* Osaka : Buraku Kaiho Kenkyusho, 1977.
This book includes inter alia, chapters on the historical background, the social class and minority status, the Buraku ghettos and the current liberation activities.

ZIENGENHALS, Walter E. *Urban Churches in Transition.* New York, Philadelphia : Pilgrim Press, 1978.
The author uses a detailed history of one particular parish in Chicago as a basis for both theological and sociological reflections on its racial transition.